PLANTS & GARDENS

BROOKLYN BOTANIC GARDEN RECORD

GARDENING
IN THE
SHADE

1990

Brooklyn Botanic Garden

STAFF FOR THE ORIGINAL EDITION:

HAROLD EPSTEIN, GUEST EDITOR

MARJORIE J. DIETZ, ASSOCIATE EDITOR

STAFF FOR THE REVISED EDITION:

BARBARA B. PESCH, DIRECTOR OF PUBLICATIONS

JANET MARINELLI, ASSOCIATE EDITOR

AND THE EDITORIAL COMMITTEE OF THE BROOKLYN BOTANIC GARDEN

ELENA BURINSKAS, ART DIRECTOR

JUDITH D. ZUK, PRESIDENT, BROOKLYN BOTANIC GARDEN

ELIZABETH SCHOLTZ, DIRECTOR EMERITUS, BROOKLYN BOTANIC GARDEN

STEPHEN K-M. TIM, VICE PRESIDENT, SCIENCE & PUBLICATIONS

COVER PHOTOGRAPH BY CHRISTINE M. DOUGLAS
PHOTOS BY ELVIN MCDONALD EXCEPT WHERE NOTED
PRINTED AT SCIENCE PRESS, EPHRATA, PENNSYLVANIA

Plants and Gardens, Brooklyn Botanic Garden Record (ISSN 0362-5850) is published quarterly at 1000 Washington Ave., Brooklyn, N.Y. 11225, by the **Brooklyn Botanic Garden, Inc**. Second-class postage paid at Brooklyn, N.Y., and at additional mailing offices. Subscription included in Botanic Garden membership dues ($25.00 per year), which includes newsletters, announcements and plant dividends.

ISBN #0-945352-31-X

PLANTS & GARDENS

BROOKLYN BOTANIC GARDEN RECORD

GARDENING IN THE SHADE

Revised edition of Vol. 25, No. 3 Handbook #61

■

CONTENTS

LETTER FROM THE BROOKLYN BOTANIC GARDEN

The pages that follow deal with growing plants in the shade, and I would like to say a few things about environmental factors and plant growth.

Of all the external influences that affect the growth of green (chlorophyll-bearing) plants, it seems safe to say that light — or lack of it — deserves the closest attention. To be sure, no plant will grow without water and adequate mineral nutrition; and no plant on earth can escape the effects of gravity. Nor can a plant be grown successfully at unusually low or unusually high temperatures. Yet we find plants growing either in or on the fringe of inhospitable deserts where both lack of water and extremes of temperature bring cultural hardship for every living thing. So, too, do we find a few green plants on the desolate Antarctic continent, and on the island of Spitsbergen a few hundred miles from the North Pole. Closer home, most kinds of plants grow with surprising vigor in the polluted air of our great cities. Life — its very essence — is at once a precious yet tenacious quality of that great and diverse category of things we say are "living." What green plants definitely cannot do is to live and grow in the absence of light.

The success of greenness comes down to the single fact that only chlorophyll-bearing plants can trap the energy that streams from the sun. Let no man underestimate this remarkable quality of the plants that cover a goodly portion of our earth. The further fact that some plants require less light than others is not particularly surprising; it is a matter of efficiency, a built-in genetic characteristic that enables some plants to live, grow and reproduce with a minimum supply of energy from the sun. The shade-loving (or shall we call them shade-tolerant) plants that are the subject of this handbook are only the shade-loving plants that belong in gardens, in our esthetic life. Some of them succeed happily, if one may use that word about a plant, on as little as one-tenth the light needed by sun-loving species.

Guest Editor Harold Epstein has gardened in the shade of great oaks for many years, so he writes from long experience on a subject that has interested him deeply. And the authors he has invited to collaborate with him in putting together this remarkable guide book are also highly knowledgeable people. Mark their every word!

GEORGE S. AVERY
Director Emeritus

One of the things that captivated me about my Brooklyn apartment when I first saw it was its small backyard, a cool green oasis in the middle of the city shaded by a magnificent old wild cherry (*Prunus serotina*). Having always gardened in sunny places, however, I was utterly unprepared for the challenges — and the pleasures — of growing plants in the shade.

The first winter at my new house I scoured the nursery catalogs for plants said to tolerate "partial sun" — surely I could cheat a bit and the plants would never know it! One soggy growing season later, most of them had succumbed to rot, and the rest looked pretty pathetic. It was time for another tack.

This time I tried plants more suited to shade — hostas, astilbes, *Bergenia*, ferns. The results were much more satisfactory and in a few spots even spectacular.

Lately I find myself eager to learn all I can about the native flora of my small part of the great Eastern forest and to recreate a patch of woodland in my yard. I've become even more aware of how precious the few remaining natural areas are — and how important it is for us to protect them.

As you peruse these pages, you'll notice that many of the plants recommended for any shady garden are natives. As gardeners, we can do our part to insure that natural areas survive — and with them the wildflowers that will grace future gardens — by buying native plants only from dealers who can guarantee that they are nursery propagated and grown, not plundered from the wild.

JANET MARINELLI
Associate Editor

■

THE ENVIRONMENT OF SHADE

GUSTAV A. L. MEHLQUIST

The word shade, when applied to gardens and gardening, has different meaning to different people. To chrysanthemum growers, the word shade is likely to bring to mind pulling black cloth over benches or beds of plants late in the afternoon to shorten the day and thus hasten flowering. To nurserymen, the word shade may mean the reduction of light intensity on young plants or on plants just dug for sale, or it may mean the necessity of providing suitable conditions for so-called shade-loving plants. The term shade-loving is used advisedly here, for although every gardener knows that many plants in nature are found in shade, and often in shade only, there is no proof that these plants actually require shade per se.

The fact that many alpine plants in nature are found on lofty mountain peaks only in strong sunlight, but in cultivation near sea level can be grown successfully only under degrees of shade, suggests that light is not the limiting factor. At higher elevations full light intensity is rarely combined with high temperatures, but at lower elevations the same light intensity may be accompanied by very high temperatures, suggesting that temperature may be the limiting factor.

Recent innovations in cooling greenhouses are now permitting operators to grow plants under glass during the summer with much less shade than before. They are thus in effect exposing the plants to much higher light intensities than before and with unmistakably better results.

GUSTAV A. L. MEHLQUIST, *Professor Emeritus of Plant Breeding, University of Connecticut, Storrs, Connecticut, is a hybridizer of carnations, delphiniums, rhododendrons and orchids.*

Also, many so-called shade-loving plants in gardens endure and often do better under much higher light intensities than those prevailing where the plants are growing wild. The common mountain-laurel (*Kalmia latifolia*) and many orchids are examples of this. In this case the fact that these plants in nature are usually found only in shade appears to be concerned with their reproduction. Although they may grow and flower very well in the garden, and also in nature in full sun when the tree cover is removed, there are seldom many seedlings to be seen, whereas in a shady location they may occur in abundance.

It is now well known that the distribution of a species in nature is limited by the conditions which permit reproduction, rather than the growing and flowering of mature plants. In the garden, where one starts with mature or near-mature plants, success may not only be possible but often more readily obtainable under conditions of higher light intensities, higher temperatures or less water.

That many plants in cultivation are adapted for a more favorable climate than that in which they are found in nature is further borne out by epiphytic plants in general, and particularly those in the bromeliad and orchid families. Members of these families often grow much better under cultivation than in their natural habitat. The explanation here seems to be that only under the relatively meager conditions of the epiphytic habitat can these plants hold their own, so to speak, against other plants which under more favorable conditions would outgrow them.

Often it may be desirable to provide some shade even at the expense of a few flowers. Many rhododendron species and hybrids will produce somewhat fewer flowers in partial shade but the flowers last much longer and the colors do not fade so fast, so the net effect is that of a "better and longer show."

Shade from Trees

It has been pointed out that the shade provided by trees may be different in quality from that provided by artificial means. It is true that light filtered through a canopy of green leaves may be different in quality from that caused by a building, or coming through a screen of wood laths or other objects. It has yet to be proved that the light coming through a canopy of green leaves is really better for the plants growing beneath, but the effect certainly is usually a more pleasing one.

With this in mind one might do well to give some thought to the selection of trees which are to provide the shade. Trees which cast a very dense shade are usually less desirable than those of more open habit. Also trees with the lowest branches some distance above ground are preferable to those with branches close to the ground, as "high" branches provide a condition akin to a "moving" shade. The plants are exposed to strong light, perhaps full sunlight, for a few minutes and then shade for a few minutes, giving an alternating play of light and shadow. Some trees, such as the European beech and most maples, provide not only too dense shade, but also have very fibrous, surface root systems which provide too much competition to smaller plants for both water and nutrients. Trees which keep their leaves rather late in the autumn provide some protection against early frosts, a feature which may prolong the season of fall-blooming herbaceous plants by two or three weeks. As a protection for rhododendrons and similar plants, high-branched conifers are hard to beat.

Of course, many people do not have the opportunity to choose their trees (shade gardening is often just making-do with what one has inherited), but those who do should endeavor to select trees with deep, coarse root systems rather than fibrous surface roots. It is probably true that a plant can be found that will grow in the driest and darkest corner, but generally speaking, the plants with the showiest flowers and foliage are most readily grown where there is fairly good light and a soil relatively free from competitive roots. Partial to light shade should be the aim, for under such conditions one can not only grow a great number of interesting plants but man, beast and fowl will be able to enjoy them.❖

BROAD-LEAVED EVERGREENS

GORDON E. JONES

Rhododendrons produce the most flower buds when trees are trimmed high, so that light filters through at least part of the day.

Shaded areas of the garden are frequently considered plant-selection problems by new homeowners who have not yet become acquainted with the many kinds of broad-leaved evergreen shrubs. Most of these plants demand some degree of shade, and it is safe to say that one exists for almost every kind of shade situation. Generally speaking, the shrubs with the largest leaves need or can tolerate the greatest amount of shade; the smaller-leaved shrubs need less shade and for best flowering performance need a goodly portion of sunshine during the day.

Broad-leaved evergreens include rhododendrons and evergreen azaleas, camellias and mountain-laurel, all famed for their superb flower displays in spring, as well as hollies, evergreen barberries, andromeda, and many others valued mainly for their foliage. All are outstanding candidates for the shaded garden, no matter how limited or

therefore more suitable for limited suburban properties. 'Dora Amateis', a recent hybrid, remains a dwarf, rich green-foliaged plant that, in early May, literally smothers itself with blooms larger than those usually seen among the small-leaved rhododendrons. 'Windbeam' is another profuse-flowering Carolina hybrid. Its flowers open white and change to delicate pink. 'Wyanokie', with

Holly, left, is prized for its attractive foliage and red berries.
Below, rhododendrons in bloom and a glade of ferns make a spectacular spring display.

extensive it may be. They are especially fine planted in woodlands under deciduous trees, such as oaks. Few plants flower properly in dense shade, though, and broad-leaved evergreens, especially rhododendrons planted beneath large trees, produce the most flower buds when the trees are trimmed high, so that light—even sunshine—filters through for a portion of each day.

Rhododendrons

Although there are many, many species, hybrids and varieties of the rhododendron, a very old favorite, the native Carolina rhododendron (*Rhododendron carolinianum*), remains popular to this day. It has neat foliage, lovely white-to-pink flowers in May, and a compact habit of growth. The plants increase in size slowly, but eventually reach 5 or 6 feet or more and nearly as wide, so this ultimate size should be kept in mind when planting them.

Some Carolina hybrids, which have smaller-leaved, dwarf species as one parent, are decidedly more compact in size and

pure white flowers, is similar but more compact in habit, reaching only 2 to 2-1/2 feet in ten years.

Two very different varieties developed from the Carolina rhododendron are 'Purple Gem' and 'Ramapo'. Both are dwarf and compact, and have very small gray-green leaves. Flowers are bright violet-blue. 'Purple Gem' is a little deeper in color and slightly larger.

The early yellow-flowered species from Japan, *Rhododendron keiskei*, is a welcome early spring delight and is especially suited to a shady area in the garden.

GORDON E. JONES, *Director of Planting Fields Arboretum, Oyster Bay, New York, is Guest Editor of the BBG Handbook,* Rhododendrons and Their Relatives.

Rhododendron

need at least partial shade to prevent their flower colors from fading.

Rhododendrons and azaleas need a soil that is at least slightly acid, and prefer one which is loose, rich in organic matter, moisture-retentive but well-drained.

Mountain-laurels and Hollies

Mountain-laurel (*Kalmia latifolia*), a native shrub common throughout woodlands of eastern North America, is not only beautiful in flower in mid-June, but is a handsome evergreen plant throughout the year. Flowers vary in color from white to various shades of pink. A few nurserymen are now propagating selected plants that produce flowers unusually and strikingly deep pink, nearly approaching red in color.

A relatively new species introduced in recent years from Japan, *Rhododendron yakusimanum*, is a slow growing, compact plant having handsome leaves with a colorful brownish-orange, feltlike indumentum on the underside of each leaf. It produces lovely apple-blossom-pink-and-white flowers in mid-May. A mature plant of this species is one of the most beautiful and highly prized specimens found in a rhododendron buff's garden.

Evergreen azaleas offer nearly as many possibilities for shade gardening as the generally larger-leaved rhododendrons. Many of the delicate pastel as well as even the strong, vibrant red and orange colors among azaleas tend to streak or fade if the plants are exposed to too many hours of direct sunshine. Many of the late spring azaleas, such as the Gumpo group and the low-growing variety 'Balsaminaeflora', definitely

Hollies are a versatile group of plants, growing under all types of conditions, including heavy shade. Many are trees, while others retain shrub growth habits. Some hollies are very hardy while others, including the English and Chinese hollies, are more tender, but are well worth trying in protected locations in the North. Among the English hollies (*Ilex aquifolium*), only the hardiest varieties are recommended for the Long Island and metropolitan areas.

'Camelliaefolia' and 'James Esson' as well as a hardy male flowering variety, 'T. H. Everett', have proven the most satisfactory in my opinion.

A hybrid resulting from crossing *Ilex aquifolium* and *I. pernyi*, an attractive small-leaf species from China, has resulted in two outstandingly hardy ornamental hollies. Smaller in leaf size than English holly, but equally lustrous and attractive, the variety 'San Jose' is a prolific berry producer, the fruits persisting well into winter. 'Gable's Male', originated by Joseph Gable in Stewartstown, Pa., is an excellent landscape plant.

The foliage of our native American holly (*Ilex opaca*) is not as glossy as the English holly but its red berries are equally attractive. The hardiest superior fruiting varieties such as 'Manig', 'Farage', 'Hedgeholly', 'Miss Helen', 'Old Heavyberry', 'Arden' or 'Canary', which has yellow berries, are extremely attractive shrubs or small trees in any garden.

Ilex cornuta, the Chinese holly, is one of the handsomest hollies, striking because of its exceedingly glossy leaves and their unusual rectangular shape with prominent but limited spines. *Ilex cornuta* 'Rotunda' and the variety 'Dwarf Burford' are fine new, low-growing types. A sheltered location must be provided to prevent winter injury.

A valuable native species of the eastern United States, inkberry (*Ilex glabra*), is a light, graceful shrub, 6 to 8 feet tall, producing black berries. Its hardiness and informal habit contribute to its usefulness as a choice shrub for shady, moist locations. There is an interesting white-berried form, *I. glabra* 'Ivory Queen', that is well worth seeking out.

Barberries

The evergreen barberries, even though armed with thorns, are excellent shrubs if kept away from edges of walks or other pedestrian traffic areas. Chenault barberry (*Berberis* x *chenaultii*), pale-leaf barberry (*B. candidula*), and warty barberry (*B. verruculosa*) are superb evergreen shrubs. Each species develops compact, low-growing plants having interesting, leathery evergreen foliage. The leaves are white underneath and make a distinct and effective contrast with the lustrous green above. The small, golden-yellow flowers in May, while not spectacular, are attractive when seen at close hand, and develop into blue-black fruits in the fall

Andromeda

Perhaps one of the most effective and reliable evergreen shrubs in shady areas are the several forms of the Japanese andromeda (*Pieris japonica*). The nodding clusters of flower buds are interesting throughout fall

Broad-leaved Laurel (Kalmia latifolia)

and winter. They open in mid-April as attractive, waxy clear white flowers similar in size and shape to those of blueberries. The young new leaves are rich coppery-bronze in spring, later turning a lustrous deep green.

A slow-growing, compact form of Japanese andromeda, (*P. japonica* 'Compacta') is available in some nurseries. The form 'Dorothy Wyckoff' develops especially large flower clusters that are pink in bud. Its foliage turns bronzy green in winter. Interesting too, especially in shady locations, is the variegated form (*P. japonica* 'Variegata').

The native mountain andromeda (*Pieris floribunda*) is more winter hardy than Japanese andromeda, but gardeners often report unexplainable difficulty in establishing plants in locations which should be ideal growing sites.

When successfully established, the mountain andromeda's prolific erect flower clusters in April are most effective and make worthwhile the effort to procure and establish this handsome species.

Abelia and Mahonia

Flowering effectively from mid-summer until frost with small, white, pink-blushed tubular flowers, the glossy abelia (*Abelia grandiflora*) is a graceful, light-textured shrub useful and handsome in shaded situations. Evergreen throughout the year in Washington, D.C. and farther south, there is usually partial defoliation and tip die-back from winter injury in more northern areas. This is not a serious flaw as the roots are dependably hardy, and after any winter-injured portions are removed in spring, abelia soon begins its amazingly prolonged flower display.

Mahonias have hollylike lustrous leaves, bright yellow flowers in clusters early in May, and blue or blue-black grapelike berries in summer. The Oregon holly-grape (*Mahonia aquifolium*), a native shrub of the Pacific Northwest, is versatile and ornamental and grows especially well in partial shade. Providing shelter from winter sun and wind will help prevent browning and winter injury to the leaves, which normally turn to a lovely bronzy-purple color in the fall. Holly-grape grows 3 to 3-1/2 feet in height and can be kept low and bushy by careful pruning. Plants spread by underground stolons, forming large clumps when growing conditions are favorable.

The leatherleaf mahonia (*Mahonia bealei*), introduced to this country from China, is an unusually different and striking plant with large, stiffly leathery, compound leaves 12 to 15 inches long on erect stems, usually 4 to 6 feet high, occasionally taller. The stout, rigidly horizontal leaves are unique in character and provide a bold texture and appearance in the landscape. The flowers are lemon yellow, somewhat fragrant and are borne in pyramidal clusters in early May. They are followed by bluish black, grapelike berries in summer. The leaves, unlike those of Oregon holly-grape, do not change color in the fall.

Leucothoe

Leucothoes are recommended as excellent companion shrubs among rhododendrons, andromedas, mountain laurel and other ericaceous or acid-soil plants. Drooping leucothoe (*Leucothoe fontanesiana*, formerly *L. catesbaei*) is a gracefully arching and spreading shrub normally about 3 feet high.

One of the most effective and reliable evergreen shrubs in shady areas is the Japanese andromeda. Shown here is Pieris japonica *'Forest Flame'.*

Its lustrous dark green leaves through the summer turn a beautiful bronze in fall, and remain attractive throughout the winter unless exposed to severe drying winter winds. Its flowers in late May or early June are small, waxy-white and fragrant, hanging attractively in 3-inch racemes along the underside of the branches.

Coast leucothoe (*Leucothoe axillaris*) is much like drooping leucothoe except that it is smaller, growing to 2 feet in height at most. Its leaves are smaller and narrower, and have a fine texture. Both species are very valuable and are attractive blending shrubs in the landscape. To keep plants growing vigorously it is advisable to prune out older stems occasionally. This can well be accomplished by cutting branches when evergreen foliage is needed in flower arrangements. The bronzy foliage in fall blends beautifully with chrysanthemums.

Cherry-laurel

One of the most satisfactory evergreen shrubs for shady conditions is Schipka cherry-laurel (*Prunus laurocerasus* var. *schipkaensis*). Hardier than the species, this variety's shiny, leathery, lustrous rich green leaves add sparkle and highlights of interest in a shaded area. Horizontal in branching habit, the verdant plants are extremely attractive year-round. Its flowers are white and carried in racemes 2 to 5 inches long coming into bloom late in May.

Camellias

Until recent years it was believed impossible to successfully grow *Camellia japonica* plants outdoors in the Long Island and metropolitan New York area. Fortunately some varieties have been found to be fairly hardy when placed in sheltered and well-protected locations offering a microclimate favorable to these handsome shrubs. Some summer shade and protection from winter sun and wind are essential. If one is fortunate to have a favorable site it is challenging to try growing a few *Camellia japonica* varieties. Flower buds may be injured some winters, but the plants will come through often with only minor injury once established. Worth trying are the pink varieties, 'Kumasaka', and 'Lady Clare'; 'Mathotiana' and 'Professor C. S. Sargent' are good reds; 'Purity' is a fine white variety. (*Editor's note:* A plant of 'Sweetheart', a pink

Camellia japonica

Camellia japonica variety, which grows in East Hampton, Long Island, has suffered total winter injury to its buds in only one winter out of twelve.)

Camellia sasanqua varieties, thought once to be promising on Long Island, unfortunately, have so far not proven to be winter hardy except in Brooklyn.

Cyrilla

A native shrub of the South, leatherwood (*Cyrilla racemiflora*) is an unusually attractive semi-evergreen shrub having pendulous clusters of small white flowers late in June or July. It is particularly distinctive and most striking in its brilliant orange and scarlet foliage color in autumn. Not commonly found in nurseries and garden centers in the New York area, it nonetheless should be sought as an interesting and worthwhile plant for shady garden areas. It requires a soil rich in humus and one that retains moisture.

A Low Evergreen

Last, though it should hardly be considered insignificant, is the low-growing *Paxistima canbyi*, a native of eastern North American woodlands. It is an evergreen, its needle-like leaves measuring less than 1 inch in length. The plants are shrubby, rarely exceeding a height of 12 inches. Although they spread by underground runners to form a fairly dense ground cover in shade, the effect is always tidy. The spelling of the generic name is sometimes misspelled, *Pachistima*. ❖

M O S S   G A R D E N S

Moss gardens are relatively rare in this country, but a notable one exists in the Japanese garden in Portland, Oregon. Even in the favorably moist Oregon climate an automatic fogging system has been found necessary for the best growth of the mosses. The Japanese have always appreciated the beauty of mosses, and the art of moss gardening has reached high development in their country. The greater use of moss has a future in Western-style gardens. Most mosses are very beautiful, and are nature's own plant selections for various shady situations. They are worth a trial, especially in shaded rock gardens and near pools.

MARJORIE DIETZ

SHRUBS FOR SHADY PLACES

HERMAN S. PORTER

Lacecap hydrangea, right, and hortensia hydrangea, far right, are a traditional choice for the shade garden.

Much of the beauty of our landscapes is created by contrasts of light and shadow as they are filtered over lawn and garden. And deciduous shrubs can be a part of these patterns, although under the most difficult conditions of shade gardening, certain shrubs may have to be tried on a win-or-lose basis.

The amount of shade that shrubs must endure in a given location is not usually the only obstacle that they face. Often there is the question of root competition from existing trees such as beech, Norway or sugar maple, which have such dense surface root systems that only the strongest-rooted shrubs can survive. More often, it is a matter of soil—its structure and organic composition, its pH, its moisture-holding capacity in relation to the needs of the plant. Before planting any deciduous shrubs in shady situations, such existing conditions should be considered.

Most gardeners want seasonal changes in their shrubs: flowers in spring, summer or autumn; appealing foliage all through the growing season and, preferably, delightful autumn coloration. In winter, they wish to see a plant with interesting form, bark or twigs that please the eye, and showy fruit that attracts winter birds. Obviously, few plants can furnish all these desirable characteristics, especially shrubs that will grow in the shade. Compromises must be made.

Too often shrubs are planted and forgotten. Shrubs are kept at their best by being given attention frequently. It is difficult to restore shrubs to their original beauty after neglect. Shrubs grown in the shade prove this rule rather than being its exception.

Shrubs in the shade require pruning to keep them within bounds and to maintain their beauty of form, feeding to help keep them healthy and luxuriant in appearance, and spraying or dusting to protect them from insects and diseases—the same as other plants. Watering is especially important during periods of drought when tree roots and shrub roots must compete for the small amount of water available.

Among deciduous shrubs there are just a few that will thrive in dense shade. However, the number that will tolerate moderate-to-light shade is considerably greater. The following deciduous shrubs will grow in varying degrees of shade. Those best adapted to dense shade are indicated by an asterisk (*). Zones are those of the Arnold Arboretum Zone Map.

*Abelia grandiflora (Glossy Abelia) 5-6 feet. A semi-evergreen shrub with small, glossy dark green leaves. Flowers white, flushed pink from June to September. Two dwarf forms, 'Edward Goucher' and 'Sherwoodii', are available. Both have flowers deeper pink than the species. Zone 6 to 5B.

*Abeliophyllum distichum (Korean Abelialeaf. Often called white-forsythia) 3-5 feet. White flowers along stems appear before leaves in late April and May. Moderate to light shade. Zone 5.

*Aronia arbutifolia (Red Chokeberry) 5-6 feet. Attractive, abundant red berries persist through the winter. Red foliage in autumn. Growth habit irregular. Tolerates moist soil. Zone 4.

Aronia melanocarpa (Black Chokeberry) 3-4 feet. Leaves light green. Fruit glossy black. Foliage purple in autumn. Shapely plant for use in border. Tolerates moist soil. Zone 4.

HERMAN S. PORTER, *now semi-retired, serves as Consulting Arborist for the Bartlett Tree Research Laboratories in Charlotte, North Carolina. He is a past president of the New Jersey Federation of Shade Tree Commissions.*

Fothergilla

Azalea See *Rhododendron.*

***Berberis thunbergii** (Japanese Barberry) 4-5 feet. Bright green leaves which turn red in autumn. Bright red berries persist through most of winter. A dwarf form 'Minor' is one of several available selections. Zone 5.

Callicarpa dichotoma (Korean Jewel-berry) 4-5 feet. A plant highly prized for its abundant violet-lavender berries which appear in late summer. Zone 5 to 4B.

Callicarpa japonica (Japanese Jewel-berry) 4 feet. Showy violet berries in October. Zone 5.

Ceanothus x delilianus (Ceanothus) 4-5 feet. Tender. Semi-evergreen. Flowers shaded to deep blue. Plant in protected locations. Zone 6.

Chamaedaphne calyculata (Leatherleaf) 1-3 feet. Semi-evergreen. Needs a moist, acid soil. Zone 3.

Clethra alnifolia (Sweet Pepperbush) 3-6 feet. Very fragrant, abundant white-racemed flowers in summer. Zone 3.

Cotoneaster dammeri (Bearberry Cotoneaster) 6-8 inches. A prostrate semi-evergreen shrub that makes an excellent ground cover. Red berries in autumn. Zone 5.

Cotoneaster dielsianus (Diel's Cotoneaster) 5-6 feet. An attractive arching shrub with red berries and small glossy dark green leaves which turn red in autumn. Zone 5.

***Diervilla sessilifolia** (Bush-honeysuckle) 3-4 feet. A yellow-flowered shrub closely related to and resembling weigela. Well adapted to shady places. Zone 4.

Enkianthus campanulatus (Redvein Enkianthus) 6-20 feet. Choice shrub in heath family bearing cream or yellow flower bells with red veins in late spring. Branches in tiers. Foliage turns red and orange in fall. Fine companion for azaleas. Zone 5.

Enkianthus perulatus (White Enkianthus) 5-6 feet. An attractive and early blooming shrub with white bell-shaped flowers. Upright habit. Zone 5.

Fothergilla gardenii (Dwarf Fothergilla) 3-5 feet. Interesting shrub that produces showy blooms of white spiked flowers in May. Leaves turn from yellow to orange in autumn. A worthy plant for any lightly shaded garden. Zone 5.

Hamamelis japonica (Japanese Witch-hazel) 6-15 feet. Midwinter flowers with yellow, twisted petals. Mild fragrance. Moderate shade. Zone 5.

Hamamelis mollis (Chinese Witch-hazel) 6-20 feet. As sensational as preceding species because of its fragrant winter flowers, usually from mid-January through February in New York City area. Zone 5.

Hamamelis virginiana (Common Witch-hazel) 6-8 feet. Bright yellow flowers in autumn at same time the leaves turn yellow. Less showy than preceding two species. Zone 4.

Hydrangea arborescens 'Grandiflora' (Hills-of-Snow) 3-5 feet. Mid-summer show from rounded heads of white flowers. Zone 4.

Hydrangea quercifolia (Oakleaf Hydrangea) 3-4 feet. Interesting foliage. Large panicles of white flowers in late spring. Withstands moderate shade. Zone 5.

Hypericum calycinum (St. Johnswort) 1 foot. Almost evergreen with very deep green leaves. Exceedingly bright yellow flowers 2-3 inches across during summer months. Zone 5 to 4B.

Ilex verticillata (Black-alder) 5-6 feet. Highly desirable shrub with red berries that persist through much of the winter. Female plants bear berries but male pollinator is needed. Zone 3.

Ligustrum obtusifolium 'Regelianum' (Regal Privet) 5-6 feet. Used largely because of its good foliage and ability to withstand heavy shade. Zone 5.

Rhododendron (Azalea) Deciduous azaleas have requirements similar to those of the evergreen species and do well in moderate shade if planted in an acid soil containing ample organic material. Most will live, though they will not flower as well, in dense shade. Among them are the following species (there are numerous hybrids and named varieties derived from them):

	Considered Hardy to Zone
R. arborescens	4
R. calendulaceum	5
R. japonicum	5
R. molle	5
R. mucronulatum	4
R. periclymenoides	3
R. prinophyllum	3
R. schlippenbachii	4
R. vaseyi	4
R. viscosum	3

Rhodotypos scandens (Jetbead) 4 feet. Large (2-inch) white flowers in May and June followed by shiny black fruits that stay on all winter. Zone 4.

Vaccinium corymbosum

Stephanandra incisa **'Crispa'** (Cutleaf Stephanandra 3-4 feet. An interesting, beautiful spreading shrub with deeply cut leaves of distinctive habit. Greenish-white flowers in June and its orange-reddish color in autumn make it even more appealing. Zone 6 to 5B.

Symphoricarpos albus laevigatus (Snowberry) 4-5 feet. An excellent shrub for dense shade. Tiny pink flowers in summer followed by large white juicy berries in autumn. Zone 3.

Symphoricarpos x *chenaultii* (Chenault Coralberry) 3-4 feet. A highly desirable shrub for the front of the border. Bears pinkish berries in late summer and autumn. Not as well adapted to heavy shade as the previous mentioned species, but it will withstand moderate shade. Zone 5.

Vaccinium corymbosum (Highbush Blueberry) 6-8 feet. A desirable shrub in the garden. An abundance of small but conspicuous white-to-pinkish flowers in the spring, followed by delicious blueberries in summer. Leaves turn brilliant orange-scarlet in autumn. Zone 3.

Viburnum acerifolium (Dockmackie) 4-5 feet. A distinctive shrub that will take more than the average amount of shade. White flowers in cymes in early June followed by fruit which is red at first and then turns black. Zone 3.

Viburnum dilatatum (Linden Viburnum) 6-7 feet. Dark green foliage. Creamy-white flowers in late May or early June followed by deep crimson berries in autumn. Withstands moderate shade. Zone 5.❖

DWARF CONIFERS FOR SHADE

JOEL W. SPINGARN

The shady garden need not omit these aristocrats of the plant world. Dwarf conifers too often are absent because they are usually categorized as sun lovers, but while it may not be common knowledge, there are a number of fine, shade-tolerant conifers available. They are rare, but with a bit of searching, can be found at specialized nurseries.

Without doubt, there is no single type of plant that imparts as much enjoyment, year long, for the space it occupies. The one prerequisite—an aesthetic one—for the effective use of dwarf conifers in the shady garden is the observance of scale. It may be difficult to meet this requirement when one's projected garden area is surrounded by large, shade-casting plants. The dwarf conifer would appear absurd if planted among majestic, towering trees, in turn underplanted with giant broadleaved evergreens, but if a dwarf conifer or a group of dwarf conifers (dwarf conifers are excellent grouped together) is used as an integral part of a small garden within the framework of the larger garden containing the massive, shade-casting plants, it would then be in scale with its immediate neighbors. The small garden, in its entirety, then becomes large enough to be congruous and in scale with the whole landscape.

Dwarf conifers also belong in the shady rock garden around pools, or among groupings of low-growing plants. The effect is quite charming when the contrast in foliage texture is achieved by associating them with low-growing herbaceous material as well as with other woody plants such as dwarf alpine rhododendrons, azaleas and daphne. Floral displays are immeasurably enhanced by using needle evergreens as a foil. In addition, the presence of these plants stirs the interest of visitors. The perfection of their beauty brings an aura of "expertness" to the garden scene. Give these plants a suitable setting and background, and you will be well on the way to accomplishing a work of garden art, which, after all, is the ultimate end to any endeavor that includes planning and design.

The following kinds of conifers have been tried and are recommended for varying degrees of shade, as noted. It is advisable before growing the forms of *Chamaecyparis obtusa* and *Cryptomeria japonica* in areas of temperature extremes to check private and/or public gardens locally to determine plant hardiness. However, all of the following are hardy on the South Shore of Long Island.

················ **KEY** ················

The number after the plant name represents the degree of shade tolerance:
FULL SHADE 1; THREE QUARTERS 2; HALF 3.

Letter or letters after the plant name represent its outline as follows:
PROSTRATE-CREEPING A; REPANDENT (spreading) B; SUB-GLOBOSE C; GLOBOSE TO LOW PYRAMID D; CONICAL E; FLAT TOP—HORIZONTALLY BRANCHED F; IRREGULAR G.
The addition of an asterisk* denotes a pygmy form with an annual growth of an inch or less.

Photo by Betsy Kissam

Top: *Hinoki false-cypress,* Chamaecyparis obtusa *'Verdonii'.*
Center: *Prostrate Norway Spruce,* Picea abies *'Procumbens'.*
Bottom: *Siberian "juniper,"* Microbiota decussata with dwarf Hinoki cypress Chamaecyparis obtusa *'Nana' below.*

Chamaecyparis obtusa

'Bassett'...3C*
'Chilworth'...3C*
'Compressa'..3C*
'Contorta'..3DG
'Densa'...3C*
'Flabelliformis'...3C*
'Gracilis Nana'...3EG
'Intermedia'...3C*
'Kosteri'..3D
'Mariesii'...3D
'Nana'...3C*
'Nana compacta'...3EG
'Repens'..3B
'Rezek Dwarf'..3C*
'Spiralis'..3E*
'Stoneham'..3C*

Cryptomeria japonica

'Compressa'..3D*
'Globosa nana'...3C
'Knaptonensis'...3D
'Mejiro-sugi'..3D
'Nana Albospica'..3D
'Pygmaea'...3D
'Sekkan-sugi'...3E
'Spiralis' 3B
'Spiraliter Falcata'..3E
'Tansu'..3D*
'Vilmoriniana'..3D*
'Yatsubusa'..3D*

JOEL W. SPINGARN, *Baldwin, New York. An active member of the American Rock Garden Society, he is proprietor of a nursery specializing in dwarf conifers and Japanese maples.*

Picea abies

Picea glauca

Thujopsis dolobrata

Tsuga canadensis

❖

Chamaecyparis

22

THE LIGHT REQUIREMENTS OF DAFFODILS

GEORGE S. LEE, JR.

Daffodils are definitely not shade-loving plants and it is really not accurate to describe them even as shade-tolerant plants. (We might as well agree to call them all daffodils which is their common and correct popular name. Only when mentioning species will we speak of "narcissus," which is the botanical name [*Narcissus*]. This distinction is recommended by the American Daffodil Society.) In the wild they grow in the mountains of Spain, Portugal and northern Africa where the winters are cold and the summers hot and dry. The fact is that, as with many of the spring bulbs, shade is a condition with which daffodils have not had very much experience. The brief part of their life cycle which is spent above ground draws to a close as the new growth appears on trees and shrubs. By the time the leaves of woody plants unfold, the embryonic flowers have been formed for another year, the scales of the bulbs are packed with starch in anticipation of dormancy, and the foliage becomes limp and brown. Another year in the life of the bulb has come to an end.

While daffodils will grow in association with deciduous woody plants, they will not long survive beneath broad-leaved or coniferous evergreens. They must flower and mature in sunlight screened by nothing more opaque than the bare framework of deciduous shrubs and trees.

Most gardeners are familiar with the fact that the foliage of daffodils must be permitted to ripen and die before it is cut if the bulb is to endure. But the maturing bulbs may be subject to two other crippling conditions. The presence of nearby trees suggests the competition of roots. The severity of this competition for nourishment and moisture will depend on distance, and whether the trees are deeply rooted as in the case of the oaks, or whether they are shallow rooted as is true with beeches and maples. Bulbs may be planted rather close to the trunks of oak trees, but when it is known that the roots lie close to the surface, it is better not to plant within the drip line of the tree. A little test digging will reveal the presence of tree roots, and if they are numerous the gardener should be prepared to give supplementary feeding to the bulbs and

GEORGE S. LEE, JR. *served for many years as President of the American Daffodil Society. He was also a keen grower of rhododendrons, azaleas and wildflowers.*

occasionally to girdle the pocket or bed to cut off the new growth of roots which will be attracted by the richer soil.

Tidy gardeners are unhappy with the drying foliage of daffodils, brief as the period is, and try to conceal the evidence or divert attention by other plantings, including ground covers. The reaction of the bulbs to this interference with the fulfillment of their natural life processes will depend on several factors: the competition for food and moisture, the height of the screening plants, and weather they are evergreen. Pachysandra is a very common all-purpose plant for shade, but daffodils will not long survive its competition. Its roots and underground runners range widely and deeply and it is a heavy feeder. Above ground the growth of an established planting of pachysandra will be almost as tall as the daffodil stems and effectively serves to shade the daffodil leaves from the light they must have. The competition of English ivy and myrtle is somewhat less severe, but nevertheless it is there and the struggle for survival will eventually become evident. These three ground cover plants are all evergreen and cannot fail to cut off vital light from the daffodils.

While two plants cannot feed in the same area without competition and a resulting unfavorable effect on the weaker of the two, daffodils will tolerate some ground covers if they are deciduous, shallow-rooted and low-growing. Even at that it may be necessary to thin the covering occasionally to permit the new shoots to break through. Acceptable groundcovers would be *Phlox stolonifera*, *Tiarella cordifolia* (foam-flower), *Mazus reptans* and *Asperula odorata*.

Oddly enough, two groups of daffodils— the reds or pinks and the reversed bicolors— have opposite needs in regard to protection from or exposure to strong light. Nearly all of the red, orange, or pink coloring in daffodil varieties has been derived from

24

Narcissus poeticus poetarum, a poet's narcissus with a small cup stained deep red, or from *N. pseudonarcissus alpestris,* which, strangely enough, is pure white. In their hybrids the coloring tends to be unstable and bleaching of the red element is not uncommon. The degree will be influenced by many factors, such as location, variety, and exposure. Reds and pinks are less affected in England and the Pacific Northwest than they are in areas where the sun is stronger. 'Rustom Pasha' is relatively colorfast, but 'Lady Kesteven' will burn within a few hours after the sun has reached it. Improvement is gradually being made, but in general flowers with red, orange, or pink coloring, especially where the color is confined to a narrow band on the cup, should be cut rather promptly after opening if the flower is to be used for exhibition or decoration where full strength of the color is important.

On the other hand, the reversed bicolors which have become so popular as a result of the work of Grant E. Mitsch of Canby, Oregon, require a good deal of strong light to achieve good color effect. To be classified as a reversed bicolor, the flower must have a colored perianth—usually yellow—and the corona (cup or trumpet) should be white. But in fact the corona invariably opens with some degree of coloring which can be eliminated through bleaching, and this requires exposure to strong light, sometimes over a period of several days. Even then the perfect contrast of colored perianth and white corona may not be completely achieved. Manipulating and stabilizing the color characteristics is not easy.

Another daffodil trait in relation to source of light—and one with which many gardeners are not familiar—is that the open flower tends to face the strongest light. So it is not uncommon that bulbs, otherwise carefully planted, will produce flowers which turn their backs on the viewer. Normally this humor of the flower can be considered in advance of planting the bulbs; if not, the flowers will give their decision at blooming time and it may not be quite what one expected!

One final effect of the intensity of light upon this daffodil concerns the time of flowering, and this effect may be used to extend the blooming period considerably. The first daffodils, and they may be had in the New York area by mid-March, may be obtained by planting early varieties in the warmer parts of the garden. These spots may be located by observing where the snow melts first. This usually results from unbroken light, a slope facing the sun, or a background which reflects heat, such as a house or wall. Conversely, the ending of the flowering season may be delayed by planting late varieties where the snow lingers. This means a barrier between the sun and the frozen ground, such as a stone wall, evergreen trees or a building. Varieties for early and late flowering are suggested below.

It is likely that some varieties of daffodils are less tolerant of shaded situations than others, but there is little testimony on the question. Commercial plantings are invariably in full sun to obtain maximum growth, and the extensive research in connection with the commercial production of bulbs, which is carried on in England, Holland and the Pacific Northwest, has not included the effects of shade. It is known that 'King Alfred', the most widely grown of any daffodil, does not flower well except in full sun and the same seems to be true of 'Carlton', another widely grown variety. While nearly all daffodils will perform satisfactorily when grown in association with deciduous trees, failure to flower well, if it is not obviously due to overcrowding and the need to divide a clump, can often be corrected by placing bulbs in a sunnier location. Daffodils are not gross feeders, but poor soil, the competition of tree roots, and the shortened period for ripening which trees create, all suggest generous annual feeding. Commercial bulb fertilizers are satisfactory, but expensive. Equally good results can be obtained from potato fertilizers which are obtainable from farm suppliers in rural areas. A high content of potash is the critical factor and a good mix can be made at home from more or less equal parts of superphosphate or bone meal, and unleached fireplace ashes, the latter supplying the potash.

Gardeners who are not familiar with variety names will find any of the following both high in quality and moderate in price. The grouping is according to the official classification of the Royal Horticultural Society and covers the entire range of varieties. Early varieties are identified by (E), late, by (L).

Daffodil bulbs need not be expensive and may be bought from local suppliers who usually carry the vigorous Dutch garden varieties or by mail from catalog dealers. The latter often carry a wider range of both garden and exhibition types, which may be either expensive or moderately priced, depending on how long the variety has been on the market. A prize-winning variety which may have been introduced fifteen years ago for $25 a bulb may now be available for 45 cents.

Trumpets

1a, yellow—Arctic Gold, Grapefruit (E), Kingscourt, Unsurpassable

1b, white and yellow—Content, Effective, Preamble, Trousseau (E)

1c, white—Ardclinis, Beersheba, Mount Hood

1d, yellow and white—Spellbinder

Large Cups

2a, yellow—Carlton (E), Galway (E), Golden Torch

2a, yellow and orange or red—Armada (E), Ceylon (E), Fortune (E), Narvik

2b, white and yellow—Daisy Schaffer, Duke of Windsor, Polindra

2b, white and orange or red—Kilworth, Selma Lagerlof, Semper Avanti

2c, white—Ludlow, Truth (E)

2d, yellow and white—Binkie

Small Cups

3a, yellow and orange or red—Ardour, Ballysillan (E), Edward Buxton, Chungking

3b, white and yellow—Angeline, Bithynia (L)

3b, white and orange or red—Blarney (L), Kanasa, La Riante

3c, white—Bryher (L), Chinese White, Cushendall (L)

Doubles

4—Gay Time, White Lion, Yellow Cheerfulness (L)

Triandrus Hybrids

5a, large cup—Thalia, Tresamble, Rippling Waters

5b, small cup—Dawn, Thoughtful (L)

Cyclamineus Hybrids

6a, large cup—Charity May, Dove Wings, February Gold (E)

6b, small cup—Beryl

Jonquil Hybrids

7a, large cup—Golden Goblet, Sweetness

7b, small cup—Cherie, Tittle Tattle (L), Trevithian

Tazetta Hybrids

8—Geranium, Martha Washington, Scarlet Gem

Poeticus Hybrids

9—Actaea, Cantabile (L)

Species

10—*N. asturiensis, N. jonquilla, N. rupicola*

Split-Corona Daffodils

11—Evolution, Gold Collar, Split ❖

27

Hardy Bulbs for Three Seasons of C·O·L·O·R

Gertrude S. Wister

All the hardy bulbs (and some are technically corms or tubers) I consider here must have a fair amount of sun or light during the time when their foliage is in active growth. They are of value for those places that have light during the winter and spring, until leaves are well grown on deciduous trees and shrubs. They are not for thick plantings of evergreens where little light penetrates. Nor will they thrive under such trees as Norway maples and horsechestnuts, which have heavy crowns of foliage and masses of surface roots. But they will grow where they are shaded by a building if there is good reflected light from open sky.

In addition to their light requirements, these bulbs need well-drained, reasonably fertile soil. It is a good idea to have their locations marked to keep the bulbs from unintentional injury while they are dormant.

Most of the bulbs are small and of great value in bringing spring to the garden or woodland early. (Daffodils appear in a separate article on page 23.) I have grouped them according to their approximate season of bloom, so the same genus sometimes

GERTRUDE S. WISTER, *Swarthmore, Pennsylvania, is a seasoned grower of many kinds of plants and is an active member of the Pennsylvania Horticultural Society. She is the author of* Hardy Garden Bulbs *(E. P. Dutton & Co., New York).*

appears in more than one seasonal grouping. South of Philadelphia, these groups are stretched further apart, and farther north, they tend to be pushed closer together.

Earliest to Bloom

These welcome flowers can be used in wooded areas, among shrubs and under small, flowering trees. A south-facing slope or a spot by a house wall that catches winter sun, no matter how shady in summer, will bring them out as early as late January, but late February and March is their usual time in the Philadelphia area.

Crocuses: Crocus species are smaller in flower than the well-known Dutch crocuses. There are many that bloom in spring; I have room to mention but three. Rodents (mice, rabbits) love them. Planting the bulbs close to the stems of deciduous shrubs gives them something of a buffer from rabbits. Cover the corms about 2 inches.

- *Crocus chrysanthus.* 4 inches. Golden rounded flowers. There are many fine varieties.

- *Crocus sieberi.* 4 inches. Plump flowers of medium violet. Vigorous.

- *Crocus tomasinianus.* 4 inches. Slender, pale lilac flowers, deeper colored within.

English bluebells are set off by deep-pink-blooming azalea.

Indispensable for its ability to increase by seed and offsets, thus keeping ahead of the rodents. Also good are its varieties 'Barr's Purple' and 'Taplow Ruby'.

Snowdrops: The white pendent flowers, one to a stem, give a good contrast to crocuses. Long-lived, increasing into large clumps. Cover about 2 inches.

• *Galanthus elwesii.* Giant Snowdrop. 8 inches. Earlier than the common snowdrop, with larger leaves and flowers, though hardly a giant.

• *Galanthus nivalis.* Common Snowdrop. 5 inches. Thrives in light woodlands. These two snowdrops are so easy and permanent they should be used by the hundred.

Winter aconite: Like short-stemmed, bright yellow buttercups with finely cut leaves. Buy only in late summer or early fall (unless freshly dug plants can be obtained) as the tubers become drier, harder and weaker the longer they are out of the ground. Soak for twenty-four hours, plant immediately, and keep ground moist for their first autumn. Cover 2 to 3 inches.

• *Eranthis hyemalis.* 4 inches. This common species of winter aconite seeds freely. The

flowers are about an inch across. 'Tubergenii', 'Tubergen's Glory' and 'Guinea Gold' are sterile hybrids that bloom a little later with large, more deeply colored flowers.

Mid-spring

Here there is an overlap with the earliest, and perhaps some bulbs should be in that group. The division into blooming seasons is only approximate. In general, March is the month of the earliest group in the Philadelphia area; April is the month of this group.

Anemones: Windflowers. Like winter aconite, they belong to the buttercup family, but look more like daisies with pretty, finely cut foliage. They require early purchase, twenty-four-hour soaking in water, and prompt planting in soil kept damp their first season. Cover 2 inches. They are grateful for summer shade, and seed freely in light woodlands. Best shielded from north winds.

• *Anemone apennina.* 7 inches. Soft blue-violet. Increases well.

29

- *Anemone blanda.* 5 inches. A little earlier, with flowers a little larger (almost 2 inches across) in blue-violet. Also to be had in white and pink. Blooms freely; seeds widely.

Chionodoxa: Glory-of-the-Snow. Hardy and dependable; bulbs increase freely. Keep species well separated from each other if their identities are to be maintained, as they hybridize readily. Cover 2 or 3 inches.

- *Chionodoxa sardensis.* 4 to 5 inches. About six starry flowers about an inch across to a stem, soft, bright blue-violet with a white eye. There is a fine white form.

- *Chionodoxa luciliae.* 4 to 5 inches. More slender than C. gigantea. A loose spike of up to ten flowers, soft, bright blue-violet, somewhat variable, with white center. Graceful, prolific, utterly charming. Indispensable.

- *Chionodoxa sardensis.* 4 to 5 inches. Up to six or more small flowers of intensely bright violet-blue flowers, tiny white eye.

Dutch Crocuses: Well known, in their color range of white, yellow and deep violet to lavender blues. Like the crocus species, they can be used among shrubs and flowering trees. They do not seem as appropriate for woodland gardens.

Erythronium: Adder's-tongue, Dogtooth-violet, Trout-lily. 6 to 12 inches. Not easy. One to several pendent flowers to a stem, like small Turkscap lilies, in white cream yellow, rose, pink or lilac. Some have handsomely mottled leaves. They need light to medium shade, and soil rich in humus, well drained, but not subject to drying out. Plant immediately; cover 3 inches.

Iris: The small bulbous iris need good drainage, winter-wind protection, and a site that is apt to be dry in summer. Cover 3 inches.

- *Iris reticulata.* 5 inches. Deep violet flowers. Not every garden suits it, but when it

is pleased, it increases well. There are a number of hybrids and varieties from light violet-blue to deep red-purple.

Puschkinia: *Puschkinia scilloides.* 6 inches. Eight or more starry flowers to a stem, looking like a small hyacinth. White with blue lines. Prefers summer shade.

Scilla: Squill. 4 to 6 inches. Hardy and indispensable. Bulbs, which increase well, are quite permanent. Cover 2 inches.

- *Scilla bifolia.* Perhaps should be in earlier group. Rather starry and wispy, chiefly in

tints of violet-blue, but there are pink and white varieties. Seeds freely.

- *Scilla sibirica.* Intense violet-blue; not quite a true blue. Three to five drooping flowers to a stem. Worth trying under trees where nothing else will grow. It may become necessary to weed seedlings out of other small plants. There is a good white form. The sterile 'Spring Beauty' is taller and a little more violet.

Late Spring

Summer Snowflake: *Leucojum aestivum.* 10 inches. About five green-tipped white bells spray out from the top of the stem. The variety 'Gravetye' is taller, with larger bells about three-quarters of an inch across. Long-lived.

Wood-hyacinths or Wood Bluebells. Usually listed under *Scilla,* but correct generic name now is *Endymion.* A fine group, handicapped by name problems. Especially good in medium shade. Bulbs increase well, persist indefinitely. (Not to be confused with the non-bulbous bluebells which belong to *Campanula*.) Cover 4 inches.

• *Scilla campanulata* (*Endymion hispanicus*). Spanish Bluebell. Ten to 20 bells on a stem 12 to 15 inches high, giving the effect of a rather loose spire of Dutch hyacinth. Soft violet-blue is the basic color; there are varieties from deep to pale violet-blue, in white, and lilac-pink.

• *Scilla nutans* (*Endymion non-scriptus*). English Bluebell. A slender, slightly smaller version of the Spanish bluebell. Less robust and showy, but nevertheless persistent.

Summer

Lilies: Two of our native lilies grow well in light-to-medium shade in rich, well-drained soil that does not dry out. Cover 3 inches.

• *Lilium canadense*. Canada Lily. To 6 feet. Leafy stalks bear up to 20 down-facing recurved flowers, pale yellow to light orange, in midsummer.

• *Lilium superbum*. Turkscap Lily. Flowers resemble the Canada lily, but are orange to red, and the petals are more reflexed, giving a more open flower. Midsummer.

Lycoris squamigera: Hardy-amaryllis. The foliage, resembling that of daffodils, appears in early spring, and disappears at the end of June. Up to seven lavender-pink, fragrant, lilylike flowers appear in early August at the top of a 2- to 3-foot stem. Long-lasting and prolific in good soil. Thrives in semi-shade. Cover 4 inches.

Autumn

Colchicum: Like large crocuses up to 9 inches high. The large, broad leaves appear in early spring, and become a nuisance before they mature and dry up in late June. The large

corms are poisonous, and left alone by rodents. Flowers, in variations of rosy purple, often lightly checkered, or white, appear in profusion in autumn. They can be planted in ground covers of ivy, pachysandra or vinca, or any light-to-medium shade where the ripening leaves will not be a problem. *Colchicum autumnale* and its white form are most often offered. Handsomer are *C. speciosum* and its very beautiful white form, and its variety *bornmuelleri*, earlier, and with a large white center; also a number of named varieties. Planting time is August or September. Cover 4 inches.

Crocus: Fall crocuses are dainty little things like the spring species. Protection from the north is desirable. There are no yellows. They range from pinkish-purples to lavender-blues and whites. Cover 2 to 3 inches.

• *Crocus speciosus*. 4 inches. A fine lavender-blue. There are good varieties, including a fine white. Prolific if the rodents spare it.

• Other good ones include *C. kotschyanus* (*zonatus*), pale rosy lilac; *C. medius*, medium purple; *C. longiflorus*, paler purple; *C. laevigatus*, early winter.

Cyclamen: Not easy to suit. They need shelter from cold winds, good soil that does not dry out, shade in summer, and sun in winter, when the foliage is very attractive. Just cover the tubers lightly with soil, and add an inch of leafmold as a mulch. *Cyclamen neapolitanum* is the best to try first. The flowers are rosy miniatures of the florist's cyclamen about 3 inches high. The leaves are marbled with silver. Plant the smooth, rounded side of this species down. Be sure to get plump tubers as early in fall as possible, or get freshly dug plants in summer from the Pacific Northwest by airmail.

A last warning on all these plants. Remember that their foliage must not be removed until it has turned yellow and rather dry.

Tender Bulbs for Summer Color

❁ ❁ ❁ ❁ ❁ ❁ ❁ ❁ ❁ ❁ ❁ ❁ ❁ ❁ ❁

John Philip Baumgardt

Zephyranthes

JOHN PHILIP BAUMGARDT, *Kansas City, Missouri. A landscape consultant and skilled grower with varied interests, he has contributed many articles to national publications. He is the author of* Bulbs for Summer Bloom *(Hawthorn Books, New York) and* Hanging Plants for Home, Terrace and Garden *(Simon & Schuster, N. Y.), and past editor of "American Horticulturist."*

To paraphrase Lewis Carroll's Red Queen, when I say "tender bulb," I mean any bulb, corm, tuber or tuberous root that is not reliably hardy in my Zone 5 garden. Flowers of plants that grow from a sort of underground storage organ often have a luminescence and carrying power lacking in other plants. For the shady garden these glowing flowers and the bold foliage of others take on special meaning. They light up the gloom; their boldness overrides the diffidence of the more delicate ferns, astilbes and other reliable shady garden plants. They become an added texture.

Caladium x hortulanum

Lazy gardeners often avoid tender bulbs. I find the idea of planting one and bringing in five (with no income tax) appealing. But you do not have to bring these indoors in the fall. Plant them, enjoy their beauty for a season, and let winter take them. You can buy more next spring. While this is not my way of gardening, I condone it when it encourages someone to plant a group of ornamental plants he has been avoiding. When he falls in love with his calla lily, he will take steps to save it.

Caladium and aluminum plant

The Quality of Shade: Shade is another of those indefinite garden terms. The shade under a high, arching elm tree differs considerably from the shade under a low, spreading maple or horse-chestnut. Under the elm, shade is protection from direct sunlight, but with full daylight. Under the low, dense tree it is shady *and dark*; light is greatly reduced. Native lady's slippers, wild-ginger, trailing-arbutus and the hellebores grow and bloom in very low light. But the tender bulbous plants want only protection from the sun's rays; they want full daylight, and most thrive on a little early morning and late afternoon sunlight.

Soils: Bulbous plants do not

Tuberous begonia

tolerate root competition; they will grow under deep-rooted trees, on the shady sides of buildings and in the lee of the garden wall only so long as the ground is unencumbered by roots of other species. This is easy because, as these are reset each spring, you may spade deeply to remove encroaching roots. Excellent drainage is a requirement of most of this group of plants, though elephant's ear and calla lily will grow in water or at a pond margin. The others want a very porous, quick-draining soil that is typically "woodsy," that is, with a high humus content, circumneutral tending toward the acid side, and loose. They all need weekly water if rainfall is insufficient to keep the soil damp under the surface layer. Feed them as growth begins and until flowering is over; then let them slow down, preparing for a dormant period.

Exposure: Tender bulbs are damaged by wind; caladium foliage becomes frayed and tattered, begonia blossoms drop, stems of achimines become kinked. Plant them where the prevailing summer wind cannot damage them; as most are relatively low, sometimes it is possible to plant a temporary windbreak for their protection. In my cutting bed a row of castor bean plants provides shade and wind shelter for the ornithogalums and shade-loving annuals.

Kinds to Grow

Achimenes: These Central American gesneriads tolerate no chill. Start the tubers indoors, barely covered, in a flat of 2 parts each peat moss and loam, one part each leafmold and sand. Water moderately at first, freely when growth is active. Transplant into light shade or even where they receive only noon-time shade. Perfect for edging and low massing (set them 9 inches apart), these foot-high plants bloom freely from early summer until frost. Give liquid manure or fish emulsion solution monthly until August. Lift in autumn. Store in clumps of dry soil in a paper bag. Propagate by breaking old tubers in two or three pieces. Easy from seed, achimenes bloom the second year. The only serious pest is the slug.

Begonia: Tuberous begonias, widely grown for their magnificent, continuously produced blossoms, have been developed from six Peruvian and Bolivian species. Press tubers into a shallow flat of damp peat moss or fine leafmold (some specialists start them upside down) and barely cover, two months before outdoor planting time. When well rooted, move to 4-inch pots filled with a mixture of 2 parts each leafmold and soil and one part each dried cow manure and fine sand. Keep moderately damp and give liquid fertilizer (fish emulsion is my preference) and grow in bright light, no direct sun, until outdoor planting time. Transplant to the garden; taller cultivars need immediate staking. They want bright light, even a little early or late sun; they do not tolerate deep shade or darkness. Water to keep the soil barely moist; feed frequently until late summer. If basal rot or mildew becomes a problem, grow drier and water only by surface irrigation. Spray with Actidione PM or Karathane. Protect from slugs and snails as these pests can devastate a planting very quickly. Withhold water a month before frost and when leaves yellow lift with soil, keep dry, and after the tubers have ripened, store in paper bags, or clean the tubers and store in peat moss in the basement. Propagate by halving large tubers two or three days prior to

rooting; sow seed (under fluorescent lights or in a greenhouse, at 68 degrees F.) six months before planting-out time.

A wide range of cultivars is now available; for garden bedding the cluster-blooming kinds make the best showing. Purchase only plump, unscarred tubers; avoid shrivelled or injured ones.

Caladiums: Deserving wider garden use, these South American arums are valuable for their showy leaves. Buy plants started in a greenhouse or dormant tuberous roots. Start dormant tubers the same way as tuberous begonias, or pot up directly in 4-inch pots in a mixture of equal parts garden loam, coarse peat moss (damp), leafmold, composted manure and fine sand. I prefer to invert the tuber, covering to a depth of 2 inches, as more sprouts—and more leaves—result. Keep barely damp until growth is active, then water freely, and give mild liquid fertilizer twice each month through late summer. Move these to the border when the weather is quite warm. Caladium beds must always be moist. A shady garden planted entirely with *C. x hortulanum* 'Candidum' (white foliage with green veins) is cool and inviting; the colored-leaf forms bring life and excitement to even a somber garden. In early fall lift with a clump of soil, compress gently, and lay to dry in a shady, frost-free place; cut off dried foliage and store in a moderately warm basement. Propagate by dividing tuberous roots several days prior to replanting. Watch for slugs.

Colocasia: The familiar elephant's ear is *Colocasia antiquorum* from the East Indies; occasionally specialists offer *C. esculenta*, taro root, which is often available locally in Spanish American vegetable markets. Handle the tubers like caladiums, or plant directly in the garden when the soil has warmed up. Allow plenty of room, give full light, even a little direct sun, and keep very moist once growth has begun. For largest leaves feed weekly with dilute liquid fertilizer—I prefer liquid manure or fish emulsion solution. Cut to the ground when frost injures the foliage and allow the roots to cure in the soil for two or three weeks; lift with a ball of soil, dry and store in sawdust, vermiculite or in a paper bag in the basement. Propagate by severing offset tubers in the spring. From Zone 6 southward, cover deeply with garden debris over winter; they will survive without lifting.

Ornithogalum: We know these bulbs as European and African relatives of the invasive little star-of-Bethlehem that grew in grandma's garden. Plant bulbs of *O. arabicum, O. lacteum, O. nutans* and its variety *boucheanum,* and *O. narbonense* and its variety *O. pyramidale* when the ground is workable in early spring; they want only dappled shade and soil deeply prepared with well composted barnyard manure, or garden compost enriched and restacked briefly with a generous amount of 5-10-5 fertilizer and bonemeal. The widest part of the bulb should be 3-4 inches below the surface. They need good drainage; water weekly when leaves appear and feed with very dilute liquid fertilizer twice monthly. Space bulbs 9 inches to a foot apart to make a display bed, or space more widely and interplant with violas or the new, very low impatiens varieties. Most of these ornithogalums send up 18-inch to 2-foot stalks, and the blooms hold very well so long as they are protected from wind. After light frost lift, clean the bulbs, cut back the tops, and store in vermiculite or perlite in a cool basement. In spring pull off and plant separately offset bulbs.

Zantedeschia: Calla lilies (arums, in England) are easy; they grow in sun or shade (not dark), damp soils or standing in 6 inches of water. Their "bulb" is a tuberous rootstock; for bog gardens, plant the dormant root, covering to a depth of 2 inches, in mid-spring; for shady gardens start indoors six weeks before frost-free date; set one per pot, using equal parts of garden loam, old cow manure (compost is a poor substitute) and coarse sand. Water once, then no more until the shoot appears. Keep moderately moist; set out when the garden is warm, and, when established, push with weekly feedings of liquid fertilizer. A clump of half a dozen white calla lilies, *Z. aethiopica,* is magnificent; for contrast, set nearby a broader planting of the lower-growing *Z. elliottiana* with white-spotted leaves and butter-yellow trumpets. The new *Z. rehmannii* hybrids come in shades of pink and bronze; they are handsome little fellows, seldom attaining 18 inches. The white-flowering cultivar 'Crowborough' is hardy through Zone 5. Lift calla lilies in a clump of soil, air dry, and store over winter in a cool, frost-free place.

Zephyranthes: Tiny zephyr-lilies make clumps and patches at the margin of my woodland garden. And every time it rains, or when I water, a new flush of blossoms appears. I plant the bulbs, covering with about 3 inches of soil, spaced every 4-5 inches, in mid-spring (they tolerate light frost) at the edge of shady patches. And that's all. With frequent watering, they are almost always in blossom; if the soil is fairly dry, bloom is sparse. As they are planted in rich soil, no additional fertilizing is required. In late fall lift the bulbs and let them dry—the foliage is very slow to shrivel, so after a couple of weeks cut it back to the top of the bulb. Store dry in a paper bag in a cool, frost-free place. Pull apart offset bulbs and plant separately. My main crop is *Z. grandiflora,* with a 3-inch, brilliantly pink trumpet on a 9-inch stem; but I grow several others including *Z. atamasco,* the atamasco-lily of Virginia, and *Z. citrina,* a small clear yellow species. ✪

ANNUALS IN THE SHADE

ROBERT P. WINTZ

roviding color in shady gardens poses a serious problem to many gardeners. What to do to add "a patch of blue" to an otherwise dreary location? To many, especially beginning gardeners, the answer may lie in the use of annuals—short-lived plants with extreme versatility, variable characteristics and wide color range.

The term annual plants is often used simultaneously or interchangeably with the term bedding plants, both referring to plants used for a single season's growth. Annuals started in the commercial greenhouse and sold to the consumer in early spring as young started plants are commonly referred to as bedding plants, as opposed to plants started directly from seed in the garden. Shade-loving annuals are usually difficult to start by direct seeding in the garden. Therefore, they are either grown on by the amateur gardener in a greenhouse, window or coldframe or purchased as bedding plants from the commercial grower at the proper planting time outdoors.

How to define shade? There is shade from buildings, shade from trees and shade from other plantings. Some shade is referred to as dense, some as heavy, and some as light. There is morning sun, afternoon sun, no sun. There is full shade, half shade, no shade. This term becomes quite relative, mainly to the individual and his own particular circumstances. You may have similar situations of shade, but one location may benefit from reflected light, another may be exposed to harsh winds, another may suffer

ROBERT P. WINTZ *is Vice President of the Chicago Horticultural Society. He is closely involved with Chicago's highly regarded flower shows and is also a maker of award-winning films for the Society.*

Coleus, right, available in vibrant colors, is one of the most reliable annuals for very dense shade. Above is Impatiens 'African Queen'.

from air pocketing and poor circulation. You must study your situation and be prepared to do some experimenting on your own.

In reviewing statistical data as to the amount of seed and plants sold, there are three annuals for shade that stand out above all others. They are "the big three"— begonias, impatiens, coleus. The impatiens (*Impatiens walleriana*), more commonly called patience plant, is one of the most dependable of all flowering annuals for shade. Much breeding work has been done over the past few years with impatiens, so that today you have a plant that is quite different from its ancestors. The old impatiens grew rather tall and leggy, with spare bloom.

Today's model is dwarf in habit and free blooming. Notable among the new varieties are inbred selections with bright satiny blooms on dwarf 10- to 12-inch plants. Examples are Blaze, a bright orange-scarlet with contrasting dark foliage; Dwarf Bright Orange, with sparkling orange flowers; and A-Go-Go, a unique, colorful, red and white bicolor, the first variegated impatiens. Newly introduced are the F1 hybrid Elfin impatiens—the most dwarf and free-blooming strain yet developed. A mass planting of these impatiens hybrids is quite a sight to behold, even in a fairly heavily shaded location.

Equally dependable for bloom and habit are the bedding or wax begonias (*Begonia semperflorens*), with foliage in many cases as colorful as the bloom. Subject to much hybridization in recent years, begonias have been bred to be sun tolerant, as well as shade tolerant. They are totally reliable, all-round good annual plants. Choose from dwarf and semidwarf forms with flowers in shades of pink, rose, red and white, and either green or bronze foliage. Favorite varieties include Pink Pearl, a dwarf pink with green leaves; White Tausendschon, a dwarf pure white with green leaves; Red Tausendschon, a semidwarf, clear red with green foliage; and Red Comet, a dwarf red with bronze foliage.

Rounding out "the big three" for shade is coleus (*Coleus blumei*). Through careful selection, varieties have been developed that are true to type and color from seed. Thus you can have plants for mass planting or combination planting that are dependably uniform. Selections are available in vibrant shades of rose, red and scarlet, as well as the popular green and ivory (Candidum) and other bi- and tricolor combinations of all these shades. Of "the big three," coleus is perhaps the most reliable for very dense shade.

OTHER ANNUAL PLANTS THAT DO WELL IN MEDIUM TO LIGHT SHADE INCLUDE:

Anchusa

Lunaria

Balsam

Lupine

Browallia

Myosotis

Calendula

Schizanthus

Centaurea

Sweet-alyssum

English Daisy

Thunbergia

Euphorbia

Torenia

Lobelia

Vinca

Normally an edging plant, sweet-alyssum will survive in a shady location, but the amount of bloom will reduce as the degree of shade increases. Therefore, don't expect the bloom to be uniform when used in a border that runs from sun to shade. For uniform bloom in a border, it would be better to use a wax begonia.

Garden balsam (*Impatiens balsamina*) is a close cousin to the patience plant, both being in the same genus. New forms are more dwarf in habit, with considerably more bloom. Browallia and torenia are two less-known annuals that should be more widely grown. Both have delicate and unusual flower forms and colors, and are suitable in beds or hanging baskets.

For that "patch of blue," it is hard to beat the ice blue shade of lobelia. Grown as a border, or in mass, the effect is always striking.

Catharanthus roseus, a tender relative of perennial ground cover *Vinca minor*, is useful with or without blooms. The foliage is rather heavy textured with an attractive sheen. The denser the shade, the fewer the blooms, but that may well not matter.

The plants that have been mentioned were selected because they are almost foolproof for a shady location. As has been discussed, there are all degrees of shade, and there are numerous other plants to try. I say try, because today with the many developments in hybridization, there are more and more plants to grow under conditions their predecessors could not manage.

Other annuals normally classified as "sun lovers," such as snapdragons, verbena, nicotiana, cleome, Drummond phlox, as well as some marigolds, are being grown with varying degrees of success.

With advances in plant breeding also come advances in growing techniques. Growing plants in containers is an example. Today's spacious patios, and indoor-outdoor rooms are especially suited to plants in containers. And not to be outdone, the modern city dweller brings the country to the city—possibly because of increased use of expanses of glass and tubbed plant material. Enterprising plantsmen are quick to call for materials to meet the need—containers that are durable and light, soil media that are rich and water retentive, plants that will flourish in confined areas. The fiberglass- and plastic-container boom is on. Today, you can buy 3-foot-diameter tubs or urns that for all the world look like concrete, yet are so light you can balance them in the palm of your hand.

Furthermore, they are actually more durable than concrete. Other types are available in all shapes, sizes and materials.

How does all this apply to shade gardening? It simply means that almost nothing is impossible. When grown in containers, sun lovers if moved into shade will be shade tolerant for a time. Not permanently, of course, but temporarily for the special occasion—the garden club meeting, when weekend guests drop in, for the garden party—just move them from one spot to another.

Can vegetables be grown in shade? So often, I've heard people complain that they can't grow vegetables due to a lack of sufficient sunshine. Generally speaking, this is true. Vegetables do need ample sun to produce a satisfactory crop. But again, this can be a matter of degree. By thoroughly knowing your garden situation, I feel certain there are ways you can achieve some measure of success.

Lettuce, radishes, salad onions, mustard, chard, turnips and beets are all cool-season crops that if planted early enough may develop into usable crops before the dense leaf growth of trees and shrubs in late spring. Your measure of success will depend on all other growth factors being optimum—a rich, humusy planting bed, good drainage, weed-free conditions.

Put vine crops, tomatoes and corn out of your mind—they need plenty of sun. I have had snap beans, on the other hand, produce quite well in partial shade, because I selected a heavy-yielding variety.

Growing in movable containers can also be a solution. You can grow a fine crop of kitchen herbs in a movable tub, or other container. And you can have the tomatoes you want by growing the new varieties, such as Patio, which will produce a heavy yield in a 10- or 12-inch pot. They, naturally, must be placed in a sunny location a good part of the day. ❖

FOLIAGE FEATURES IN THE SHADE

Top: Hosta montana 'Aureo-marginata' blends well with the bluish tones of Hosta 'Frances Williams' to its left.
Center: Ruffled leaves of coleus combine nicely with the pink flowers and variegated foliage of New Guinea hybrid impatiens.
Right: Feathery fronds of a tree fern contrast strikingly with the gigantic leaves of Gunnera.

40

HOSTA AND THE SHADY GARDEN

ALEX J. SUMMERS

Botanists and others have had a great game with the genus *Hosta*, changing names without regard for those already in use, or using the same name for a number of plants. Hosta, which is often called plantain-lily, is still occasionally sold as *Funkia*, a generic name which was changed in 1905! Even the great Liberty Hyde Bailey contributed to the hosta muddle by calling *H. gracillima* 'Variegated', *H.lancifolia fortis*, and then soon after applying the same name to *H. undulata erromena*.

Most people are familiar with hosta in its commoner forms, such as *H. undulata* 'Variegata' with the leaf broadly striped white in the center; *H. gracillima* 'Variegata' *cathayana*, the early-sprouting species known under a variety of incorrect names, which flowers in September; and the old-fashioned August-lily, *H. plantaginea*.

Because of the identity confusion among hosta plants, many commercial growers offer mislabelled plants and many individual plants can be bought under a variety of names. It is not unusual to find that some brand new name and a fancy price have been applied to plants which have already been in existence for some time. The future hosta buyer should beware and when possible, see the plants before buying.

As most hosta species are natives of Japan (and a few of China and Korea), it is to be expected that the only comprehensive work on nomenclature problems regarding the hosta muddle has been done by Japanese botanists, with Dr. Fumio Maekawa's monograph of 1940 and Dr. Noboru Fujita's series of papers published in the mid 1970's the best known.

There are close to a hundred species, forms and varieties described by the Japanese. Some of the so-called species are hybrids, and many so-called varieties are garden forms and nowhere to be found in the wild. Hosta in the wilderness is a variable plant with no clear line of demarcation between one species and the next, with everything between a classification problem. To add to the confusion of the older hosta population in this country, many new plants have been imported recently from Japan, some of which are valid species collected in the wild, some divisions of selected Japanese garden seedling-grown plants. And, of course, the most baffling are the plants either received as hybrid seedlings, or grown from seed collected in Japanese gardens and producing hybrid offspring. Add to all this the many seedlings grown in this country from garden material, which often self-sows, and it is not unusual to find hosta enthusiasts with well over a hundred cultivars, most of which have names only more or less accurate, and again, subject to change!

Hosta in the Garden

Hosta ventricosa

Hosta can be divided generally into two groups; the first, those which bear seed which should be prevented from forming by removing the fading flowers to avoid self-sown seedlings, or, if a few are permitted to ripen, gathered as soon as ripe, and grown elsewhere. They may be sown in fall or spring outside, or grown under lights in the basement or in a greenhouse. Seedlings started under glass will occasionally flower the first year, but usually it takes two years for small-leaf types and longer for larger-leaf types. Self-sown seedlings should never be permitted to take over the garden as the result will soon be a jungle. The second group of hosta are those more or less sterile plants which, even though known as species, are undoubtedly of garden hybrid origin, as without seed for reproduction they could not endure in the wild. This seedless group naturally is less of a problem for the gardener who turns to hosta for permanent garden or landscape effects. For those gardeners interested in handsome foliage effects, and not particularly in the flowers as such, most of the seed-bearing hosta can be happily grown in heavy shade, where they will not flower at all (thus setting no seed) and, especially in the variegated leaf forms, light up such dark and often neglected areas with gleams of silver or gold.

Hosta may again be divided into size groups and indeed must be so that proper placement is insured. Certainly the wee ones must be kept from hiding behind the giant ones. All the tiny hosta are new to this country with the early flowering *H. nakaiana* probably the most common. It was introduced as 'Nakaimo Minor'. ('Nakaimo' is a larger-leaved plant, apparently a hybrid with *H. capitata* influence.) Another early flowering tiny hosta, smaller than *H. nakaiana*, is *H. venusta*. Both of these will rebloom and this year *H. venusta* was seldom without a flower spike—if a 10-inch spike can be called that. As both these species set seed profusely, many hybrids are being grown, often with quite large leaves, indicating cross-pollination with large-leaf types. Other small-leaf, later-flowering species are *H. gracillima* and a wee plant from Saishu Island called 'Yaku Giboshi.' This last forms a flat wheel-like arrangement of elongated narrow leaves often veined with yellow and flowering in September. *H.*

ALEX J. SUMMERS, *Roslyn, New York, is a former president of the American Hosta Society. He is a landscape consultant and nurseryman.*

gracillima also flowers at this time. It has slightly larger leaves held from the ground, although also spreading. The old *H. sieboldii* has produced some seedlings more variegated than itself and, in one case, a mutation or sport also more centrally variegated. These variegated gems, due to lessened amounts of chlorophyll, are appreciably smaller than the parents and should be fascinating for the shady rock garden. One seedling of *albo-marginata* has appeared with a nice gold edge, a distinct contrast with its white-edged parent. Small variegated-leaved plants will soon be plentiful, as many retain variegation from seed, particularly seedlings from 'Beatrice'.

The medium-leaf-sized hosta have been used for edging for generations, but the two most commonly used are far from ideal for the purpose. *H. gracillima,*'Variegated', the old *lancifolia, lancifolia fortis,* among other names, seems more prone to insect attack than others, and it also has the unfortunate quality for us of turning yellow and then brown after we water the lawn on a hot day with our cold well water. Another suffering in this manner is the old *albo-minor.* Breeding has produced darker, thicker foliage and larger white bell-like flowers from *albo-minor,* but they have not been tested for cold water resistance. Just as common for edging is the variegated-center leaf *H. undulata* 'Variegata'. This has the undesirable habit of producing plain green leaves during the summer, hardly an asset. Many new hosta show interesting possibilities for border or path edgings.

There are dozens of large and giant-leaved plants (some up to 12 by 18 inches), suitable for ground cover when planted in groups, or alone as an accent. These large plants, to be effective, must have good culture and plenty of water. The giant variegated leaf-types are then garden traffic stoppers.

Aside from small- and large-leaf hosta types, both of which have plenty of variegated

A few of Hosta's *many forms. New spring growth, bottom left, is particularly sprightly. The flowers of some hostas, for example* Hosta sieboldiana, *center, are showy and some are fragrant.*

forms, there are some that are appealing for their solid blue or glaucous leaf color. One species, *H. tokudama*, is extremely blue with a round, cupped, seersucker leaf, and there are forms of other species, such as *H. sieboldiana* and *H. nigrescens*, with very blue leaves. Other species have forms with lessened amounts of grey or blue grapelike bloom on the leaves, some with more on the reverse leaf side. One with a grey-white reverse is the white-backed *H. hypoleuca.*

Fragrance is always a desirable quality, and the old-fashioned August-lily, *H. plantaginea*, is well known for it. The larger-flowered 'Grandiflora' form with flowers up to 9 inches is very elusive and the double-flowered form even more difficult to find. Fragrant hybrids are few: 'Invincible', in blue, 'So Sweet', a large flowered pure white, and 'Fragrant Bouquet' in white tinged with blue are well worth including in your collection.

Shade is essential in the summer garden for relaxation and tranquility when temperatures become too hot for garden activity. Indoor air conditioning may offer relief for some people, but the outside can also be air-conditioned. Circulation can be improved for both the comfort of people and plants, and can serve to keep out mosquitoes and lessen the slug problem. Too many gardens are closed in by dreary masses of grouped shrubs which can be functional as screens, but after a few years, become airless traps from which one wishes to escape.

So, shade should be high with openings to allow the entrance of air and light. This is the kind of shade that the perennial hosta appreciates, although hosta will adapt itself to all degrees of shade, providing soil moisture is adequate.

Perhaps the best shade is that derived from tall pines, although personally I like Japanese yew and American holly, trimmed high, for the berried effects and bird activity they create. Ideally, oak, tulip and apple trees should be avoided because of the inch-worm problem, and falling fruits from apples are an additional hazard to hosta foliage. Tulip and maple trees attract aphids and the subsequent honeydew dropped then turns to sooty mold, which disfigures all vegetation beneath.

So much for the canopy for hosta plants. Other plants I like interplanted with hosta are the fall-flowering evergreen liriopes, particularly 'Monroe's White' and the variegated-leaved 'John Burch', which has extremely dark flower stalks as well as dark flowers. Also, not to be overlooked are ferns, which blend beautifully with hosta, and may be used with them in the most delightful combinations. The Japanese painted fern is used here in quantity and is a very early indicator of drought, as it flattens out as the ground dries and becomes erect again on watering. Two precautions: Do not plant hosta in beds of ivy or pachysandra; do not use too much rough litter which may attract mice (especially the shorttailed pine mice), who find hosta roots extremely palatable.

Sources for hosta mentioned above are not plentiful. Perhaps the best plan would be to join the American Hosta Society, 5605 11th Avenue South, Birmingham, Alabama 35222. ❖

46

CHOICE PRIMULAS FOR MONTHS OF COLOR

ALICE HILLS BAYLOR

There are many locations in the shady garden where the colorful and charming members of the genus *Primula* may be planted— beside a pool or brook, along a path shaded by rhododendrons or other shrubs, under an apple tree or an evergreen, in light woodland or in partially shaded sections of the rock garden. One small planting will be the forerunner of others, for it is quite impossible to be satisfied with a few once one has successfully grown these treasures. There are hundreds of primulas and fortunately many can be grown by meeting only a few of their requirements. Others are difficult to bring into bloom as it is nearly impossible to imitate the growing conditions of their native habitat. (Perhaps this last reason is why many of us try again and again to germinate seed of these difficult species.)

The range of primrose colors is so great that any combination or blending of the many kinds can be made. Intense shades and vivid colors contrast with pastels; the cool shades seem to accentuate the brightness of their neighbors while yellow and white primroses serve to knit the garden's pattern into a harmony of tints and tones. Many members of this magnificent plant group ask only for partial summer shade, soil that has been deeply cultivated and enriched with humus and organic fertilizer, moisture during the growing and flowering season, excellent drainage, and a mulch to conserve moisture and create a cool root run.

The first requisite is partial shade. Or one might use the term "dappled shade" which suggests that primulas should have sun on their flower heads for a short period each day. They should be planted where air circulates freely as they do not like to be smothered.

When preparing the planting site, dig deeply to avoid later effort. Such thorough preparation may save the primroses during a dry period. Here at Sky Hook in Vermont, we dig two spades deep, saving the top soil in a wheelbarrow from the first

Primula japonica

ALICE HILLS BAYLOR *has recently retired as proprietor of Vermont's Sky Hook Farm, a nursery specializing in primroses.*

A spectacular mass planting of Primula malacoides.

excavation to use as the top for the last portion. The subsoil is turned and a 2- to 4-inch layer of humus (leafmold, compost or old hay) is added. The top soil from the next space is put on top of this prepared area and thus we continue. This method of preparation ensures moisture retention, adequate space for roots to run for food and an area 2 to 3 inches above the surrounding ground to give perfect drainage. The mulch, which is put on after planting, adds another 2 inches to the height of the bed. The edges of the beds in our primrose garden are low stone walls on which grow the dwarf species. In the woodland garden we use logs, which create a naturalistic scene to hold the prepared soil.

When setting out individual plants, start with a large hole as it is most important for the roots to have plenty of room when spread out. A trowel full of dry cow manure is placed at the bottom of the hole and the plant is held so that the crown is slightly above the surface of the bed and the roots not quite reaching the bottom of the hole. Soil is filled in around the roots about half way to the crown, then water is added to wash down the soil and to avoid air pockets. More soil is finally added to fill the hole. The crown of a primrose plant should not be covered with soil or mulch. If primroses are planted in this manner there is no need to remake the planting site for three or four years, unless one wishes to add to the supply by dividing the plants. When an entire area is planted it is soaked and the mulch added. If planting is done in fall an early spring mulch is advised; if in spring, mulch again in summer. This may be any good humus mixture—compost, leafmold, or ground corn cobs, peanut hulls or ground bark, to which fertilizer has been added. (*Editor's note:* The fertilizer, which is recommended for the purpose of replacing soil nitrogen temporarily lost through action of bacteria in decomposing the organic matter, can be any nitrogenous fertilizer, such as nitrate of soda, applied at rate of 1-1/2 lbs. per 100 sq. ft., or sulfate of ammonia, applied 1 lb. per 100 sq. ft.)

Perhaps more primroses have been lost in winter due to too much protective covering than not enough. They are hardy denizens of cold regions, high mountains, crevices and meadows where their long roots penetrate deep into the soil for food and moisture. The gardener can protect primroses from stinging winds with spruce or other evergreen branches (discarded Christmas trees are

48

excellent), or any material that will not pack. Avoid leaves; rather use corn stalks or spent tomato vines as a winter scarf for primroses. This type of covering will hold snow in place; when snow is lacking, it is sufficient protection. The shelter of a large rock and the coziness of a log are also to their liking.

The joy of gardening begins early as spring approaches. The first flowers are so welcome; some primulas bloom as the snow that covered them melts. The brilliant *Primula rosea grandiflora* and its smaller forms, Petite Pink and Kleinii, are miniatures and often flaunt their 3- to-6-inch cluster against winter's white blanket. For that reason they should be planted where they will be seen and appreciated when it may be difficult to venture too far into the garden. When several plants of *P. rosea* are massed together the clusters merge completely, hiding the dark green pointed foliage. A humus-enriched pocket in the rock garden, with a northeast or northwest exposure, and filled with plants of *P. rosea* will make an unforgettable picture in early spring. One should transplant or divide this little beauty very soon after blooming, as it needs time to establish its wiry roots. I learned this to my great disappointment when I divided them in early September one year and in spring found that frost had heaved them out of the ground. They may be raised from seed, which should be fresh; or the plants can be divided as *P. rosea* multiplies faster than many other primroses.

As soon as the snow melts and the warm breath of spring is in the air, the fat buds of *Primula denticulata* push up sturdy stems and soon become round flower heads of lilac to lavender, or pink, rose, red, deep purple or pure white. This early bird comes to us from the Himalayas and is one of the easiest primroses to grow. It grows readily from seed, or the old plants may be divided. There is only one special requirement to provide—

and that is drainage, for if water stands on or around the crown *P. denticulata* becomes the victim of crown rot. (When this happens the roots can be lifted, each planted separately, and a small new plant will develop.) The foliage of *P. denticulata* becomes large as the season progresses, so 6 to 8 square inches of space should be allowed. If the foliage wilts during hot summer weather, the outer leaves may be removed and the plant soaked after the sun has set.

Following on the heels of these earliest of primroses are the precious and colorful varieties and hybrids of *P. juliae*. The mass of bloom, the range of colors, both of the carpet and the stalked Julianas, repay bountifully with only a minimum of care. The species is a recent addition to the Vernal group as it was discovered in 1911 in the Eastern Terminus of the Caucasus in Asia Minor. Since then it has been hybridized with *Primula vulgaris* and *P. polyanthus* to give many hybrids. The species is a flat plant with extremely small, heart-shaped foliage and crimson flowers with a white eye. Its offspring will spread by creeping root stock and should be used as an edging, in a pocket of the shaded rock garden or beneath flowering trees or shrubs. The colors are rich crimson and burgundy, bright pink to shell pink, lavender, pale yellow to bright yellow, opal blending to pure white. The carpet types have a single flower on a stem, the stalked, a cluster of florets on a 3- to 4-inch-high stem. The roots have a tendency to come to the surface, so the fertile mulch is necessary.

Primula abschasica has been grown in this country only in recent years. The seed was sent from the Leningrad Botanical Society. Its natural station is in Abschasica in the Russian Caucasus. This species is a charming addition to the Vernal group for the wine-purple flowers bloom very early in spring and give a second flowering in fall. The rosette of leaves lies flat upon the earth and the many flowers, each on a single stem, almost completely cover the foliage. It has been crossed with *P. vulgaris* by H. Lincoln Foster, who introduced it to this country with pleasing results, for the beautiful flowers are extra large, and have a larger eye, which is rose colored.

The vernal primroses are those from the moist meadows of the British Isles and Europe. They are of the easiest culture and give to spring a wealth of bloom. The beloved English primrose, *P. vulgaris*, bears each yellow flower on a single stem. It has been crossed with a native of eastern Asia, *P. sibthorpii*, which is pink. They are colorful beauties, with flowers so abundant as to make a solid bouquet from a single plant. The other member of this group is *P. polyanthus*, which is perhaps the most popular garden primrose. It is the "bunch primrose," its cluster of flowers held on a 6- to 8-inch stem and in colors that defy description. This primrose is the result of hybridizing *P. veris* and *P. elatior* and other primroses from different parts of the world which had red, lavender and purple flowers. From these crosses, which have endured for many generations, have come primroses of "rainbow" hues. These glorious primroses bloom in May and are exceedingly spectacular.

Of the many others in the Vernal group, one or two should be mentioned. The primrose from Ireland, 'Garryarde Guinevere', will stop a garden visitor with the appeal of its outstanding form and deep bronze foliage. It is one of the most beautiful plants in its entirety because of the contrast

of pink flowers above the curled red-bronze leaves. Also of interest is the Cowichan strain of primroses, whose plants also have bronze foliage, but eyeless flowers of deep red, and of satin-substance. There have been several good color forms of the Cowichan strain hybridized in recent years. All of the many Vernal primroses multiply and can be divided in a year or two with ease to make a greater supply for one's garden.

After *P. polyanthus* has claimed the scene for about a week, the various auricula primroses open their buds to expose their distinctive velvet-textured flowers. Wild forms from the European Alps have been hybridized for over a hundred years, to produce our lovely garden auriculas. All the auricula group can be distinguished by their smooth, almost succulent, leathery leaves which can be toothed or smooth. Others have dark green or grey leaves with a farinalike coating, and a few have a white leaf margin. These mountain dwellers, which can be found growing in rocky crevices and screes, have adapted themselves to our gardens and are enduring and hardy. They ask for a top dressing of limestones or gravel over the humus-enriched soil. They also endure a sunnier location than that of other primulas. All auriculas produce side shoots which can be removed and rooted. From seed they will produce wondrous colors.

Towards the end of May while the Vernal group is still putting on a show, we at Sky Hook are drawn towards the woodland where the stately candelabra primroses are planted around three small pools connected by a tiny brook. These are the Asian primroses—from Japan and the high meadows of the

Himalayas—and extend the primrose season into June. Here the soil is woodsy, black and rich. Here the candelabras spread their broad leaves and send up the flowering stalk on which tier after tier of florets appear. *Primula japonica* is the first to come into bloom. The near side of the pool garden is planted exclusively to them. The upper reaches of this area have the white-flowered varieties, which merge into pale pink, then deep pink, with the glowing reds along the brook connecting the upper pool with the second one. They seem to wade into the water that drips from the stair-step brook and their seeds germinate on moss-covered rocks. The Oriental hybrid candelabras (those of *P. bulleyana, P. beesiana,* and *P. burmanica*) bloom a week or so later than their Japanese counterparts. Among the flower colors are pure white (Mt. Fujiyama), bright yellow (Oriental Sunshine), tangerine and vivid blends (Oriental Sunset), brilliant red (Manchu Red) and shell pink (*P. pulverulenta,* Bartley Strain, with farina-covered stems). There are also pastel, coral, pink and fuchsia varieties. They are all of easy culture and if one does not have a woodland, they are spectacular against an evergreen planting or in a nook of shrubs or beside a pool. They enjoy more moisture than the primroses mentioned, but must not be planted where water is stagnant. They may be propagated both by seed and division.

In July the belled primroses take our interest when *P. alpicola* blooms. There are three forms of this fragrant primrose with its 12- to 14-inch stem bearing a spray of nodding bell-shaped flowers. Violacea is lavender to lilac, and there is a gray one I call "Old Smoky"; the white form is lovely, and the lemon-yellow one, "the moonlight primrose of Tibet," is heavily powdered with farina. It is one of the main attractions in the garden on a summer evening. *P.*

secundiflora, from China, bears from narrow, serrated leaves a 12-stem topped with nodding clusters of colorful bell-shaped florets of rose, deep wine, or purple. The root system is much shorter than the others in this group and the foliage rosette should be ringed with small stones to keep it securely in place. It is perfectly hardy. *P. sikkimensis,* found by Hooker in Sikkim, and *P. florindae,* found by Kingdom-Ward in Tibet, are very much alike. They are both yellow, bloom together in late July or August, and have beautiful foliage, which is a garden ornament in itself. They both also have a large "sunburst" cluster of many florets, often 30 to 60 in one spray, which are delightfully fragrant. Both cross so freely with other members of this group (especially with *P. alpicola* and *P. waltonii*) that it is difficult to keep the type and many colorful hybrids are produced. All of the plants in the Sikkimensis group need deep, moist, rich soil, about a half of which should be humus. Their native homes are the wind-swept heights of the Himalayas, along streams or under the spray of waterfalls. They have conformed to the conditions of our gardens to give us a remarkable tribe of late-blooming primulas.

When the fragrant bell primroses go to seed, there is often bloom on the early Vernal group to give a garden walk a little excitement. Then in November a pink or crimson flower will lift its head above a sifting of soft snow as though to remind us that another primrose season will give us joy when the snow melts in spring. It is then we place evergreen branches over the primroses to protect them from stinging wind. The branches will also catch and hold scarlet maple or dogwood leaves to make a patchwork winter blanket.

The American Primrose Society invites membership. Write the Society, 2568 Jackson Highway, Chenalis, Washington 98532. ❖

English ivy (Hedera helix) and its many forms can be trained in a pattern up a fence or wall.

HARDY VINES FOR SHADE

Hybrid clematis does well in partial shade–even when forced to intertwine with itself on a short post.

Boston-ivy (*Parthenocissus tricuspidata*)— Evergreen vine for covering brick and masonry. Two forms, 'Lowii' and 'Beverly Brooks', have small leaves and neat habit.

Bittersweet (*Celastrus scandens*)—Suitable for semishade. Degree of fruiting decreases as shade increases. This vine is too rampant for most suburban situations.

Clematis (*Clematis*)—Most kinds of clematis will flower adequately in partial (not dense) shade, so long as the soil remains rich and reasonably moist.

Climbing Hydrangea (*Hydrangea anomala petiolaris*)—Handsome flowering vine for various degrees of shade. Clings to tree trunks.

Dutchman's-pipe (*Aristolochia macrophylla*)— A fast-growing, leafy vine suitable for screening and to provide shade for porch, trellis, arbors. It is a twining rather than clinging vine.

English Ivy (*Hedera helix*)—Standard evergreen vine for dense shade. In the North, the foliage burns badly unless plants grow against walls with northern or western exposures and are protected from strong wind. There are many varieties.

Honeysuckle (*Lonicera japonica* 'Halliana')—A rampant vine with fragrant summer flowers. A last resort for vast areas in shade.

Silver-lace Vine (*Polygonum aubertii*)—Fast growing twining vine with abundant showers of cream-colored flowers in late summer.

Virginia Creeper (*Parthenocissus quinquefolia*)—Familiar clinging vine of woodlands. It will climb stumps, rocks, tree trunks, walls, but is generally too rampant for small properties.

Wintercreeper (*Euonymus fortunei*)—An evergreen shrub or vine which clings to supports by suckerlike rootlets. There are several selections, some having variegated foliage. Most are fairly compact rather than rampant and suited to small properties. ❖

SELECTED FERNS FOR THE SHADY GARDEN

F. GORDON FOSTER

To the Botanist or gardener the words "ferns" and "shade" are almost synonymous. Although ferns are sometimes found growing in areas of full, all-day sunlight, most prefer either filtered sunlight or alternate periods of full sun and shade. Some ferns seem indifferent to soil requirements, others thrive on limestone, but the majority grow best in moist, slightly acid, loose soil.

Ferns have three major components —the leaf, rhizome and roots. Often growers classify ferns by the size and architecture of their leaves, and say little or nothing about the hidden rhizome-root system. In most Northeastern ferns the rhizome, really a modified stem, grows just beneath the surface of the ground and is never seen. In general, rhizomes fall into either one of two categories; that is, a runner or crown type. Ferns having rhizomes of the first group form good ground covers and are best planted where they will not invade other areas with their spreading habits. Crown-forming ferns continue to grow as individual plants and have little or no tendency to spread.

For garden use, ferns may be divided into three groups. First the "monarchs" consisting of the three osmundas and the ostrich fern; then the "intermediates"— shield ferns, lady ferns, hay-scented fern and others; and lastly the "miniatures"—ebony and maidenhair spleenworts, polypody, and

Ebony spleenwort, Asplenium platyneuron, grows on rocks and hillsides from Maine to Florida and westward.

fragile fern. These are just a beginning; as your garden progresses more may be added.

There are three species of the genus *Osmunda* in this area—interrupted fern, *Osmunda claytoniana*; cinnamon fern, *O. cinnamomea*; and royal fern, *O. regalis*. All are strong, stately plants, choosing moist acid soil for their habitats. They often grow 5 feet or more in height under favorable conditions. Under the drier conditions of most gardens these ferns grow about 3 feet tall. Select a damp area in the garden for the osmundas, and plant them in soil deeply mulched with oak leaves, bark, or wood chips. Allow a minimum of 3 feet between plants. All osmundas are crown formers and there will be no danger of their spreading for many years. All appear early in spring, and if kept fairly moist do not become shabby until fall.

Ostrich fern, *Matteuccia pensylvanica*, is also a crown former, but spreads by means of underground runners to form new plants. In nature it prefers an abundantly wet, marshy habitat. Kept reasonably moist in the garden it makes a beautiful stand. Because of its strong, deep root system it is especially functional where erosion is a problem, such as along the banks of a stream. Where growing conditions are ideal this species can be a rampant grower, and care must be given to its confinement.

There seems to be no limit to the selection of ferns in the intermediate-sized category. Choose some of the many shield ferns of the genus *Dryopteris;* all are crown formers and void of migratory habits. Most are about knee-high and some are evergreen, making them desirable for winter effects.

Marginal shield fern, *D. marginalis*, is a robust species and is fully evergreen. Its leaves are yellow-green in early spring and turn to dark blue-green by mid-summer. This fern has a shallow rhizome-root system and is generally found growing in shaded rocky areas and woods.

Goldie's fern, *D. goldiana*, sometimes called giant shield fern, grows shoulder-high in nature but usually reaches about half this height in the garden. Avoid planting it in natural wind passages as the leaves are brittle and break easily. It has dark brown, heavily scale-clad croziers which appear early in the spring. This fern is not evergreen and its leaves turn brown in mid-autumn. Goldie's fern looks best when used in groups of three. For maximum protection, plant it in the shelter of a large boulder.

The two spinulose ferns, *D. spinulosa* and *D. intermedia*, with their more finely cut leaves, will remain evergreen where winters are not too severe. Common with others of the genus, they have shallow rhizome-root systems and prefer a deeply mulched, rocky soil. Planting them beside large rocks or at the base of old stumps provides a natural setting.

Plant crested shield fern, *D. cristata*, where the soil is constantly damp. The leaves of this fern grow in an upright manner with leaflets almost horizontal.

Christmas fern, *Polystichum acrostichoides*, is fully evergreen regardless of the severity of the winter. Each spring its new white-scaled croziers uncurl amid the prostrate but still green leaves of the previous season. A dense stand of this species used on a slope will help solve an annoying erosion problem. There are many variations in the leaves such as color, size and degree of twisting of the pinnae; these are generally caused by ecological conditions.

No shady garden should be without the native common maidenhair, *Adiantum pedatum*. This delicate, light green fern, with its arching leaves, is among the prettiest. It is not difficult to grow provided it has loose,

F. GORDON FOSTER, *a retired engineer, is one of America's leading fern enthusiasts and the author of* Ferns to Know and Grow *(Hawthorn Books, New York).*

Photo by Stephen K.M. Tim

Top: *Ostrich fern,* Matteuccia struthiopteris, *arches over a bluestone walk.*
Above: *The native cinnamon fern,* Osmunda cinnamomea.
Opposite: *A magnificent tree fern,* Cyathea australis, *prefers some protection from the sun and considerable room to grow.*

deeply mulched soil of compost, peat moss and rotted leaves, and small stones or gravel. Keep the soil moist at all times.

The following group of ferns is often maligned because of spreading habits. When planted within confines of natural boundaries these species cause little or no problem. An occasional thinning, however, is beneficial for general well-being.

Hay-scented fern, *Dennstaedtia punctilobula,* has beautiful, feathery yellow-green leaves. It spreads rapidly but makes a dense ground cover and, while indifferent to soil conditions, its growth is accelerated in damp, loose soil. It is a good selection for shaded areas with dry, sandy soil where more choice ferns will not thrive. Leaves of the hay-scented fern are long lasting when cut and used in floral arrangements. In nature this fern is often found growing on rock outcroppings or among boulders, the latter location giving it the second common name of "boulder fern."

When carefully located, lady fern, *Athyrium filix-femina,* makes a delightful, cool-appearing, light green fern. There are many variations of this fern and all make good plants for the shady garden. Pink-stemmed lady fern, *A. filix-femina* var. *rubellum,* is a more colorful variation. All require a constantly moist, well-mulched area for best growth. Older leaves of lady ferns get shabby in late summer but new leaves continue to appear until frost.

New York fern, *Thelypteris noveboracensis,* is another one of the invasive species. It can be used to advantage between a woodland area and a lawn where its advancement can be controlled by either pulling or mowing. This fern is one of the first to turn brown in late summer.

Rock gardens, stone walls or ledges, already present or carefully planned and built, make excellent places to display the "miniatures." Maidenhair spleenwort,

Asplenium trichomanes, grows best in a limestone niche or between two stones. In nature it grows on vertical faces of rocks or cliffs, thus insuring good drainage. Walking fern, *Camptosorus rhizophyllus,* is an unusual fern. In addition to propagating by spores it also reproduces by vegetative budding on the ends of the long tapering leaves. Both species are most difficult to establish, and the latter fern is an easy prey of night-prowling slugs and snails.

The little polypody or rock-cap fern *Polypodium virginianum,* is a small evergreen fern highly suited for rocky areas. In nature it is seldom found growing directly on the ground. Select a depression in a large rock or boulder and fill with leaf mold. Keep it moist but well drained until the fern gets a foothold.

There are two native bladder ferns, fragile fern, *Cystopteris fragilis,* and bulblet bladder fern, *C. bulbifera.* Fragile fern is small and easily grown in rock crevices at the edge of stone garden steps. Bulblet bladder fern prefers a higher moist-rock position to enable its long tapering leaves to gracefully hang downward. This fern reproduces by means of spores as well as small, asexual bulblets on the underside of the leaf.

Ebony spleenwort, *Asplenium platyneuron,* looks very much like a miniature Christmas fern although there is no generic relationship. It generally grows in thickets at the edges of woods and along open roadside banks. I have also seen it lining the inside of an old farmhouse well.

Grape ferns, also among the miniature plants, divide into deciduous and evergreen groups. Rattlesnake fern, *Botrychium virginianum,* and daisy leaf fern, *B. matricariaefolium,* both deciduous, are among the first ferns up in the spring. Dissected grape fern, *B. dissectum,* and multifid grape fern, *B. multifidum,* come up in July or August and are fully evergreen, the sterile leaf

remaining until replaced by the new leaf the following year.

All grape ferns require a mycorrhizal function in the soil and are most difficult to grow in home gardens. They can be grown when carefully transplanted from one area to another of similar soil condition. Do not expect them to grow in a new location by just transplanting them in a large clump of their native soil.

Consider some of the many hardy, exotic species for the shade garden. Two of the more colorful ones are the Japanese painted fern, *Athyrium niponicum* (*A. goeringianum*), and the Japanese pink shield fern, *Dryopteris erythrosora.* The first is deciduous like our common lady fern; the second is evergreen in localities having milder winters. Each leaf of the Japanese painted fern ends in a graceful taper and the pinnae terminate in a similar manner. The rachis and midribs are wine red, with this color blending into the soft grey-green of the leaf. Japanese pink shield fern is of the same genus as our native shield ferns, and receives its common name from the little pink shields covering the spore-bearing capsules on the underside of the leaf. The shiny, bronze-green leaves of this plant make it an unusual addition to the garden.

There are also many English horticultural variants of lady ferns, hart's-tongue fern and shield ferns. Some of these have their pinnae ending in finger-tip tassels, others have beautiful leaves ending in crown-like tops. As to hardiness, all are about the same as their progenitors. *Athyrium filix-femina* 'Frizellae' has small, rounded pinnae alternately spaced, giving the leaf a spiral appearance. *A. filix-femina* 'Victoriae' has alternate pinnae pointing upward or downward, giving the leaf a criss-cross pattern. 'Acrocladon', another cultivar, has brilliant green leaves and looks somewhat like a bunch of parsley.

Our native hart's-tongue fern is now

virtually extinct, but the European species and many of the English cultivars will thrive in limestone settings.

Finally, build a rock garden or reserve a shaded area just for the summer to display tender, exotic house ferns that have been indoors all winter. This can be a highlight of the entire garden. The different davallias, maidenhairs, polypodys, pellaeas and others will not only enjoy and beautify your garden, but will return to winter house conditions as much healthier plants. ❖

Sensitive fern, Onoclea sensibilis, *is very adaptable, growing in shade and diffused sunlight.*

Ground Covers and Hardy Flowering Plants for Shade

Andre Viette

What is a ground cover? The answer often given is that it is a low, rapidly spreading, evergreen plant. But in truth, a ground cover is any plant which will cover the ground, whether its growth be by underground runners, above-ground stolons or clumps as long as they cover the surface. Grass is the most important ground cover, but it is not suitable for most shaded areas. I have seen azaleas and rhododendrons used as very effective ground covers. Ground covers can be 4 to 5 feet high, as in *Cimicifuga* and *Aruncus,* or only a few inches high, as in *Mazus* and *Ajuga.* Foliage can be evergreen or deciduous, and flowers can be insignificant or very colorful.

Certain annuals can be planted among groups of ground covers for summer color. Bulbs also add color in plantings of monotone ground covers such as pachysandra and ivy. Daffodils and *Scilla* and other spring bulbs are especially useful in combination with *Hosta,* since the leaves of *Hosta* unfold late in the spring after the bulbs have bloomed and mask the unsightly foliage of the bulbs.

ANDRE VIETTE, *Fishersville, Virginia, has presided over one of the leading collections of perennials in the United States, Martin Viette Nurseries. Among his fondest subjects are* Hemerocallis, *peonies and lilacs.*

Attractive mulches, such as bark, stone, hulls, can be used with ground covers which are deciduous and lose their foliage in winter, or those with foliage which disappears in summer, such as *Sanguinaria canadensis* (bloodroot) and *Dicentra spectabilis* (bleeding-heart). Mulches give the ground a pleasing appearance, conserve moisture and suppress weeds.

Certain ground covers are excellent for open areas which have no bounds. *Ajuga, Lamiastrum galeobdolon, Physostegia, Monarda* and *Lysimachia* are very invasive and should not be used where some semblance of order is desired. A 6-inch aluminum edging can be used to contain these rapidly spreading perennials, but eventually they will escape over it.

Such native plants as *Shortia, Mitchella, Gaultheria* and *Galax,* which have evergreen foliage, need acid soil. The plants which will tolerate more than average-moist soil conditions are: *Galax, Shortia, Athyrium, Hosta, Hemerocallis, Myosotis, Phlox divaricata, Mitchella* and *Lobelia.*

The following is a selection of perennial plants suitable for ground cover for the shade or in shaded flower gardens or naturalistic plantings. While many choice native plants, which grow naturally in woodlands, are included, space does not permit a complete listing. Others can be found in books devoted to this subject and in catalogs of

Top: *Polygonatum multiflorum*
Center: *Asarum virginicum*
Bottom: *Dicentra spectabilis*

Photo by Stephen K.M. Tim

nurseries specializing in wild flowers. Many native ferns are valuable plants for shade; see page 54.

Height—varies as to climate, soil conditions, season, rainfall and culture; and therefore, is an approximate listing.

Color—Refers to bloom and varies with acidity, rainfall, soil conditions and the age of the plant. Usually a vigorous growing plant or a young plant will produce flowers or a lighter color.

Shade—Open shade, high shade and filtered shade are designated as light. Sun all morning, and afternoon shade would fall into this group. However, an area receiving morning shade and all-afternoon sun would be considered a sunny location. Medium or moderate shade would be that area receiving little sun through the day and is typical of a heavy oak forest. Black shade, shade which occurs under maples or heavy pine forests, is not considered.

Life—A plant's longevity as a ground cover or in the garden among other plants.

Foliage—Pertains to whether a plant is evergreen or deciduous.

The term **Growth** refers to the speed with which a plant will cover the ground.

Season of bloom will vary somewhat from region to region, and can also be affected by growing conditions, moisture and other factors.

Scientific Name Common name	Height	Color	Season	Shade	Life
Aconitum carmichaelii *(fischeri)* Aconite	36 inches	Light blue	Aug., Sept.	Light	Medium
Adonis amurensis Pheasant's Eye	12 inches	Greenish- yellow	March, April	Light	Medium
Ajuga reptans Bugle, Bugleweed	2 inches	Blue	May, June	Light	Medium
Anemone hupehensis Japanese Anemone, Windflower	20 inches	Rose	Sept.- Oct.	Light	Medium
Anemone nemorosa and European Wood Anemone	2 inches	Blue, white	May	Medium	Long
Aquilegia canadensis Canada Columbine	18 inches	Red and yellow	June	Medium	Medium
Arisaema triphyllum Jack-in-the-pulpit	12 inches	Green, purplish	April-May	Medium	Long
Aruncus dioicus Goatsbeard	54 inches	Cream	June	Medium	Long
Asarum virginicum Evergreen Wild-ginger	4 to 6 inches	Brownish	May	Medium to deep	Long
Astilbe **(hybrids)** Astilbe, Spirea	6 inches	Various	May-July	Medium	Long
Aubrieta deltoidea Purple Rock Cress	4 inches	Rose, lavender, red, purple	April, May	Light	Short

Foliage	Growth	Comments
Deciduous	Moderate	An excellent companion for *Anemone japonica*, chrysanthemums and other late-blooming perennials in flower borders. Prefers a rich soil, high in humus. Naturalizes well. Roots are poisonous. Subject to cyclamen mite attacks. There are other aconites, some deeper in color and earlier blooming. Called monkshood, too.
Deciduous	Slow-moderate	Fine-textured plant for early touch of color in shade garden. Do not overwater. *Adonis amurensis* 'Florepleno' has double flowers; *A. vernalis* blooms later.
Evergreen, semi-evergreen	Fast	A leading ground cover. Spreads rapidly by stolons. Good for color contrast among rhododendrons and azaleas. Tends to die out in spots, giving seedy appearance. There are varieties with white or pink flowers, reddish or variegated foliage and other species.
Deciduous	Moderate, in clumps	Beautiful in late summer and fall flower garden. Mulch with leaves or straw in winter. *Anemone vitifolia*, 18 inches, is hardier, otherwise similar.
Deciduous	Moderate	One of the most rewarding shade plants. Delicate in both flower foliage. Naturalizes well. As foliage dies down in summer, tuberous begonias can be interplanted among it.
Deciduous	Moderate	There are many other species and varieties, most of which do best in light shade.
Deciduous	Moderate	Early spring native for medium to even dense shade. Rich, moist soil.
Deciduous	Moderate, in clumps	Large, long-lived plant for bold fernlike beauty in shade garden. Grows equally well in fairly dry woodland soil or along ponds and streams. There is a form 'Kneiffi' with finer foliage
Evergreen	Moderate	An excellent native plant. Often listed incorrectly in catalogues. Handsome foliage, but can burn during winter in cold areas. Flowers are unimportant as ornamental feature.
Deciduous	Moderate, in clumps	There are several varieties and a few low-growing species, giving a full range of heights and color. One of the choice perennials for the shaded flower garden. Rich, moist soil is essential.
Evergreen	Moderate, in clumps	Crevice or wall plant. Cut back after flowering.

continued

Scientific Name Common name	Height	Color	Season	Shade	Life
Bergenia cordifolia Siberian-tea	12 inches	Rose	April, May	Medium	Medium
Brunnera macrophylla Forget-me-not	14 inches	Blue	May, June	Light	Moderate
Caltha palustris Marsh-marigold	14 inches	Yellow	Early April	Medium	Medium
Campanula carpatica Carpathian Bluebell	8-10 inches	Blue, white	June-August	Light	Medium
Ceratostigma plumbaginoides Leadwort, Plumbago	6 inches	Deep cobalt-blue	August-September	Light	Long
Chelone obliqua Turtle-head, Shellflower	36 inches	Rose-pink	July-August	Light	Long
Chimaphila maculata Pipsissewa	5 inches	White	June-July	Medium	Long
Chrysogonum virginianum Golden Star	6 inches	Yellow August	April-	Light	Medium

Epimedium *requires little care and has been known to survive under maples where even pachysandra and myrtle have failed.*

64

Foliage	Growth	Comments
Evergreen	Large clumps	Valuable for bold effects. Winter protection needed in cold climates. Dislikes dry, sandy soil. Plant in rich, moist sites, sun or shade.
Deciduous	Clumps	Sometimes listed as *Anchusa myosotidiflora*. Useful in shaded rock garden.
Deciduous	Moderate-fast	Prefers moist, even wet soil. Dies back in summer.
Deciduous	Moderate	Suitable for light shade in rock garden or flower border.
Deciduous	Fast	Slow to start growth in spring. Flower color is exceptional.
Deciduous	Moderate-fast	Needs rich, moist soil.
Evergreen	Slow, spreading	Attractive plants for dry woodlands or shaded rock gardens where soil is acid. Hollylike foliage with white veinings.
Evergreen, semi-ever-green	Moderate-fast	Excellent for partial shade. Golden star has an exceptionally long season of bloom. Very effective in partial shade.

Sanguinaria canadensis, an Eastern woodland plant, is useful for naturalizing .
White flowers appear in April.

Photo by Stephen K-M. Tim

Scientific Name Common name	Height	Color	Season	Shade	Life
Cimicifuga racemosa Black Snakeroot	50 inches	White	July-August	Medium	Long
Convallaria majalis Lily-of-the-valley	8 inches	White	May	Light-medium	Long
Cornus canadensis Bunchberry	6 inches	White	May	Medium	Long, once established
Dicentra spectabilis Bleeding-heart	26 inches	Pink-red	May	Light	Medium
Digitalis purpurea Foxglove	48 inches	White, rose	June	Light	Short
Dodecatheon meadia Shooting Star	10 inches	White, pink	May-June	Light	Medium
Doronicum plantagineum Leopard's-bane	30-36 inches	Yellow	May-June	Light	Medium
Epigaea repens Trailing-arbutus	3 inches	White tinged pink	April-May	Light to Medium	Long
Epimedium alpinum Barrenwort	10 inches	Rose and cream	April-May	Light to Medium	Long
Filipendula vulgaris Meadowsweet	36 inches	White	July	Light	Medium

Foliage	Growth	Comments
Deciduous	Clumps	Thrives in rich, fairly moist soil. Although too tall for small flower gardens, this perennial can be enjoyed in shaded shrub borders. The flowering period is a long one, and even the beadlike flower-bud stage is effective.
Deciduous	Fast	'Fortune's Giant' is far superior to the common form, and its foliage lasts longer into the fall season. Subject to damage by spider mites.
Deciduous	Moderate, spreading	A beautiful northern native, best described as a miniature flowering dogwood. Difficult except in cool sites, in acid, rich soil, but clumps can be established and will often thrive in home gardens.
Deciduous	Moderate, in large clumps	Loses its foliage in summer. *D. eximia* has rose flowers; blooms nearly all summer. *D. cucullaria* (Dutchmans-breeches), dainty plant for shaded rockery or wildflower garden, flowers in spring, then loses its foliage.
Deciduous	Clumps	A biennial, but under some conditions, seeds itself and naturalizes. Good background plant for shaded flower border.
Deciduous	Moderate	Prefers moist, acid soil.
Deciduous	Moderate-fast	Excellent companion for ground covers, spring bulbs and other early perennials. Becomes dormant in the summer. Divide every three years after flowering. There are other species and similar named varieties.
Evergreen	Moderate, once established	Needs acid soil. Buy cutting-grown plants in pots. Flowers have delicious scent. Same plant family as *Rhododendron*.
Semi-evergreen	Spreading clumps	One of the finest, long-lived perennials for shade. It requires little care and has been known to survive under maples where pachysandra and myrtle have failed. Virtually no weeds grow through a solid bed of epimedium. The flowers in the spring are exquisite and lovely in flower arrangements where they can be appreciated at close range. In addition to *E. alpinum,* there are several other species and varieties of value: *E. grandiflorum* has large white flowers: *E.* x *youngianum* 'Roseum' (or *lilacinum*), lavender; *E. pinnatum* var. colchicum, yellow.
Deciduous	Moderate, in clumps	The doubled-flowered 'Flore Pleno' is usually grown. Fine plant for flower borders, poolsides, but needs rich, moist soil.

continued

Trillium grandiflorum, *a showy native, needs rich, moist soil.*

Scientific Name Common name	Height	Color	Season	Shade	Life
Galax aphylla Galax	6 inches	White	June	Medium	Long
Galium odoratum Sweet Woodruff	8 inches	White	May, June	Medium	Long
Gaultheria procumbens Wintergreen	5 inches	White flowers, red berries	May	Medium	Long
Geranium sanguineum Cranes-bill	14 inches	Rose	June-July	Light	Long
Hedera helix 'Baltica' Baltic English Ivy	6 inches	n/a	n/a	Medium	Long
Hedyotis caerulea Bluets	2 inches	White-blue	May-June	Light	Long
Helleborus niger Christmas-rose	15 inches	White	Dec.-Feb.	Medium.	Long

Tiarella cordifolia is a good ground cover for areas where soil remains moist.

Foliage	Growth	Comments
Evergreen	Moderate, spreading	The foliage of *Galax* is especially distinctive, making this plant one of the best for woodland gardens and other shady areas. Needs acid soil with leaf-mold or peat moss.
Deciduous	Fast	A herb whose wilted flowers and leaves have the scent of freshly cut hay and are used to flavor white wine. Fine companion for forget-me-nots and *Doronicum,* or with shrubs and spring bulbs.
Evergreen	Spreading	Hardy evergreen for colonizing in rich, acid soil. Fine woodland plant.
Deciduous	Moderate, in clumps	There are many other geraniums, some for borders or rock gardens, others for woodland.
Evergreen	Moderate-rapid	When grown as a ground cover, ivy is hardier and less subject to winter burn than when it is allowed to climb. Less hardy varieties than above will usually thrive in protected locations.
Deciduous	Rapid, clumps	Prefers cool, moist meadows or very open woodlands. Not for hot, dry locations. *H. michauxii,* a creeper for light shade; grows between flagstone.
Evergreen	Slow	Needs a rich soil. Other species include Lenten-rose (*H. orientalis*). Poisonous if eaten. Fine woodland plants.

continued

Scientific Name Common name	Height	Color	Season	Shade	Life
Hemerocallis (species and varieties) Day-lily	20-48 inches	Yellow, orange, maroon, blends	May-Aug	Light	Long
Hepatica americana Liver-leaf	5 inches	Lavender- blue	April	Medium	Long
Hesperis matronalis Sweet Rocket	36 inches	White, violet	June	Light	Medium
x Heuchera americana Alum-root	36 inches	Dull white	June	Medium	Long
Heucherella tiarelloides	16 inches	Pale pink	June-July	Light	Medium
Hosta Plantain lily	(see page 42)				
Iris cristata Crested iris	6 inches	Lilac-blue	May-June	Light	Long
Lamium maculatum Spotted Dead Nettle	8 inches	White, rose	May-July	Light to medium	Long
Liriope muscari Lily-turf	12 inches	Lilac, white	Aug.- Oct.	Light	Long
Lobelia cardinalis Cardinal Flower	36 inches	Scarlet	July-Aug.	Light	Moderate to short
Lysimachia clethroides Summer Loosestrife	36 inches	White	July-Aug.	Light	Long
Maianthemum canadense Mayflower	4 inches	White	May	Medium	Long
Mazus reptans	2 inches	Lavender	June-July	Light	Long

Foliage	Growth	Comments
Semi-ever-green to deciduous	Moderate, in large clumps	Durable perennial for a variety of conditions. Numerous hybrids and species. Quite tolerant of many kinds of shade and soil. Can be naturalized. Indispensable for summer gardens.
Evergreen	Moderate, clumps	Attractive woodland plants for rich soil. *H. acutiloba* is similar but has larger leaves.
Deciduous	Clumps	The perennial form naturalizes readily and is suitable for pool or streamside, or lightly shaded areas of flower garden. Flowers are scented.
Deciduous	Clumps	Attractive for foliage clumps.
Deciduous	Clumps	Hybrid of *Heuchera* and *Tiarella*, also listed as *Heuchera tiarelloides*.
Deciduous	Moderate, to rapid	Needs fairly moist soil. Do not mulch heavily. There are other iris species which will grow in light shade. They include *I. lacustris*, a smaller form of *I. cristata*; and *I. verna*, effective in rock gardens.
Semi-evergreen	Rapid, spreading clumps	Useful ground cover. *Lamiastrum galeobdolon (Lamium galeobdolon)* has yellow flowers and is an invasive plant, but excellent where a rapid spreading ground cover is needed in shade. It has silver and green leaves and will tol-erate poor soil. Common name is archangel. It grows 10 inches high in semi-vinelike manner and flowers in May.
Evergreen	Rapid	Rewarding ground cover for shade where hardy. Bold lilylike foliage in tufts and flowers at a time when shade area is in need of color. There are many forms, some with dark foliage or variegated.
Deciduous	Clumps	Handsome native plants for open woodland or shaded poolsides. Need moist, rich soil. Fairly easy to grow from seed. *L. siphilitica*, great blue lobelia, tolerates more shade.
Deciduous	Rapid, spreading	Excellent ground cover or in areas of shaded flower border. Spreads. *L. punctata* has yellow flowers in June-July, which last over a long period; it is also spreading and may become a nuisance in flower border unless checked. *L. nummularia*, moneywort or creeping Charlie, is a creeping plant with bright green, glistening foliage and yellow flowers, and it too can become a pest, although it makes a useful cover in large areas.
Deciduous	Fast, spreading	Colonizing native, attractive in woodlands or under trees and Canada shrubs, such as oaks, rhododendrons. Acid, moist soil, but tolerates average soil. Also called false lily-of-the-valley.
Deciduous	Rapid, creeping	One of the few plants suitable for crevices between flagstone in shade. Not always reliably hardy in very cold areas. Can become a pest in lawns.

continued

Scientific Name Common name	Height	Color	Season	Shade	Life
Mitchella repens Partridge-berry	2 inches	White flowers, red berries	May	Medium	Long
Monarda didyma Bee Balm, Bergamot	36 inches	Red, pink, lavender, salmon, white	July	Light	Long
Myosotis scorpioides Forget-me-not	6 inches	Blue	May-June	Light	Long
Pachysandra terminalis Japanese Spurge	10 inches	White	April	Medium to dense	Long
Phlox divaricata Wild Blue Phlox	12 inches	Lilac-blue	May-June	Light	Medium
Phlox stolonifera Creeping Blue Phlox	10 inches	Violet-blue	April-May	Light	Medium

Lamium maculatum 'Beacon Silver' spreads rapidly and flowers in May.

Foliage	Growth	Comments
Evergreen	Rapid in favorable sites	Prefers slightly acid to neutral soil. Once established, spreads fairly rapidly.
Deciduous	Rapid, spreading	Aromatic and attractive to butterflies and hummingbirds. Useful as background in semi-shaded areas of flower borders or naturalizing along water, by walls and fences. Likes moist, rich soil, but does well enough in average garden soil. Frequent division recommended for clumps in the flower border.
Deciduous	Spreading	Short-lived but self-sows freely in rich, moist soil. Useful by half-shaded pools, streams.
Evergreen	Moderate	The standard ground cover for shade, especially under trees. It is tough, hardy and durable, and for these reasons, should not be planted directly under broad-leaved evergreens as it removes moisture and food from soil. Spreads by branching rootstocks.
Deciduous	Moderate, clumps	Beautiful in flower border with tulips or in woodland or shaded rock garden.
Deciduous	Moderate	'Blue Ridge' is offered by nurseries. An attractive ground cover, which becomes a waving sheet of blue in the spring.

continued

Woods phlox becomes a waving sheet of blue in spring.

Scientific Name Common name	Height	Color	Season	Shade	Life
Polemonium caeruleum Jacobs-ladder	15 inches	Blue	May-June	Light	Medium
Polygonatum multiflorum Solomons-seal	30 inches	White	May	Medium to deep	Long
Primula Primrose	(See page 47)				
Pulmonaria angustifolia Lungwort	10 inches	Blue, pink buds	April-May	Light	Medium
Ranunculus aconitifolius Fair Maids of France	18 inches	White	May-July	Light	Medium
Sanguinaria canadensis Bloodroot	9 inches	White	April	Medium	Long
Shortia galacifolia Oconee Bells	8 inches	White	May	Medium	Long
Smilacina racemosa False-Solomon's-seal	36 inches	White	May	Medium	Medium-long
Symplocarpus foetidus Skunk-cabbage	36 inches	Purple, brown	March	Medium	Long
Thalictrum aquilegifolium Meadow-rue	36 inches	White, purple	June-July	Light	Long
Tiarella cordifolia Foamflower	8 inches	White	May	Light	Medium

Foliage	Growth	Comments
Deciduous	Moderate, clumps	Lovely perennial for foreground of flower garden or in woodlands near pink rhododendrons. Likes rich, fairly moist soil.
Deciduous	Moderate	A fine spring-blooming plant, with pendant white flowers, and useful in woodlands or any shady garden. It prefers light to medium shade, although it will grow in extremes of full sun or very deep shade. Soil should be moist and full of humus. The foliage is delightful with other flowers in arrangements. There is a variegated foliage form, and there are native species, which are also worthwhile.
Deciduous	Moderate, clumps	Compact, neat habit. Attractive in foreground of flower borders. *P. saccharata* 'Mrs. Moon' has deep pink flowers and spotted foliage.
Deciduous	Moderate	The double form 'Flore Pleno' is especially recommended. Also *R. acris* 'Flore Pleno' is the double form of the European field buttercup, which has yellow flowers.
Deciduous	Moderate	Usually loses its foliage in summer, especially in dry woods. An Eastern woodland plant, useful for naturalizing. There is a double-flowered form. Propagate by dividing roots after flowering.
Evergreen	Slow, spreading	A choice, hardy native for rich, acid-soil woodlands and shaded pockets in a rock garden. Well worth any extra effort when clumps flower in spring. *Shortia uniflora* is the Japanese counterpart, and is generally considered more difficult, although this is an academic problem as this species is rarely listed.
Deciduous	Moderate, spreading	Woodland plants with handsome foliage and spikes of flowers.
Deciduous	Moderate	This native of wetlands makes a handsome, leafy accent by shaded pools or in moist woods where it can be naturalized.
Deciduous	Moderate	Fernlike foliage and airy flowers. Other species of note: *T. speciosissimum*, gray foliage, fuzzy yellow flower panicles; *T. dipterocarpum* mauve flowers; *T. kiusianum*, choice carpeting plant with purple flowers, for light shade in rock garden. All need rich soil high in humus content.
Semi-evergreen	Fast	Spreads by runners. A fine ground cover for areas where soil moisture can be retained. *T. wherryi* is a superior plant for a shaded rock garden or woodland planting. The foliage is about 6 inches high, and the pale pink flowers reach a height of 10 inches in mid-May. It does not creep as does *T. cordifolia*, but needs same adequate soil moisture to thrive.

75

Scientific Name Common name	Height	Color	Season	Shade	Life
Trientalis borealis American Starflower	6 inches	White	May	Light to medium	Moderate
Trillium grandiflorum White Trillium	12 inches	White	May	Medium	Long
Trollius (hybrids) Globeflower	30 inches	Yellow, orange	May	Light	Medium
Vancouveria hexandra American Barrenwort	10 inches	White	June-July	Medium	Long
Vinca minor Periwinkle, Myrtle	4 inches	Blue, white	May-June	Light to medium	Long
Viola (species and varieties) Violet	4-12 inches	Purple-blue, white, yellow	May-June	Light	Medium
Waldsteinia fragarioides Barren-strawberry	4 inches	Yellow	July-Aug.	Medium	Medium

An evenly gold-colored plant of 'Shade Master' with promising buds already showing a lavender tint.

Foliage	Growth	Comments
Deciduous	Moderate, spreading	Delicate woodland plants of attractive form, suitable for colonizing or for shaded rock garden.
Deciduous	Moderate	A showy native to plant in woods, among ferns and shrubs, in rich, moist soil. There are many other trilliums of note. All are superior plants for the shady garden.
Deciduous	Moderate, in clumps	Needs rich, moist soil. Beautiful plants in the spring flower garden.
Deciduous	Fast, creeping	Fine carpeting plant in shade. Needs acid soil rich in humus. Use peat moss or leafmold in quantity when planting.
Evergreen	Moderate	Excellent ground cover, perhaps the best because it has evergreen leaves, but also effective blue (or white) flowers. Prepare the soil before planting by adding quantities of organic matter and water well until plants are established. Foliage is yellowish in too much sunshine.
Deciduous	Moderate to fast	Many, many kinds, and not all of them tolerate shade. Some may become weedy. Recommended for light shade (in moderate shade, fewer flowers are produced). *V. blanda* (white); *V. canadensis* (white); *V. labradorica* (deep violet); *V. pallens* (white); *V. pubescens* (yellow); *V. sororia* (dark blue); *V. striata* (cream).;
Deciduous	Moderate, creeping	Ground cover plants for shaded areas or woodlands. Rich acid soil.

Trollius ledebourii *brings bursts of color to the shady garden in spring.*

Choice Plants for the Garden in the Shade

Harold Epstein

A casual analysis of the desirable decorative plants used in our gardens reveals our dependence upon eastern Asia, and particularly Japan, as a natural source for choice plants adaptable to our Eastern climate. It was over a hundred years ago (1859) that the renowned American botanist, Asa Gray, published his classic paper which stressed the relationship of the Japanese flora to that of the eastern United States. Since that time there has been an increasing, but slow, introduction of new and dependable garden subjects available to us. Asa Gray recognized and revealed the close affinities which exist between the two geographical areas. This relationship is dependent upon a pre-glacial land connection between Asia and North America across the Bering Sea. A study of the flora of Japan and eastern United States indicates a total of thirty common genera, including *Clethra, Epigaea, Leucothoe, Pachysandra* and *Shortia*.

I have experimented for over 25 years with a large number of Japanese species in my suburban New York garden. It is interesting to note that most of the common genera are adaptable to the shady garden, and some require considerable

HAROLD EPSTEIN, *Larchmont, New York, is Guest Editor of this Handbook. An avid collector of rare plants and a world traveler as well, he is President Emeritus of the American Rock Garden Society.*

shade. There are several common genera with just two species, one in North America and another in eastern Asia.

Familiar Genera of Woodlands

Caulophyllum robustum from Japan and *C. thalictroides* from eastern North America (commonly known as blue cohosh) are very similar woodland plants of easy culture. *Diphylleia grayi* (Japan) and *D. cymosa* (eastern North America), commonly known as umbrella-leaf, are also similar plants of easy culture.

Epigaea asiatica (Japan)—This evergreen, creeping subshrub, larger in all respects than our eastern relative, *E. repens* (trailing-arbutus or May-flower) defies the general rule of adaptability to our eastern lowland climate. Several attempts at cultivating it in the open garden under very shady and protected conditions have proven futile. The plants quickly become desiccated and apparently require cool conditions and a substantial winter snow cover. It has been cultivated with moderate success in some Pacific Northwest gardens, but it appears to be intolerant of our Eastern climate. It is native to open woodlands in the mountains of the northern Island of Hokkaido, as well as northern Honshu, both areas with substantial snow cover.

Our native *E. repens* is not as difficult (for

it is a lowland plant), and it can be cultivated either from fresh seed or established cuttings. Young small seedlings can be established in an acid, peaty soil, and must not be permitted to become dry until well established. It accepts considerable shade and protection.

The *Shortia* genus has been simplified in recent years. The eastern United States species, *Shortia galacifolia* (Oconeebells) has always been thus identified except for John K. Small, who had been with the New York Botanical Garden, and who published his *Manual of the Southeastern Flora* (1933), wherein he prefers the use of the genus *Sherwoodia*. It is doubtful that other botanists have given preference to this terminology.

Shortia is a distinctive evergreen ground cover highly evaluated by most gardeners; many consider it amongst the most beautiful native plants with all-year decorative value. The decorative foliage is particularly outstanding in winter when it takes on reddish or bronzy crimson coloring. The one-inch, bell-shaped and nodding flowers vary from white to pink and appear in spring.

The Japanese members of this genus had previously been accepted in two genera, *Shortia* and *Schizocodon*. In recent years the Japanese botanist Jisaburo Ohwi simplified this classification, so that we still have *Shortia uniflora*, with the forms of *Schizocodon* now identified as *Shortia soldanelloides*. The latter species has several varieties—form *alpina*, the dwarf alpine phase; var. *minima*, a very diminutive phase from the high mountains of Yakushima; var. *magna*, a larger-leaf type; var. *ilicifolia*, a rather rare form with small leaves with teeth on upper half, from mountain woodlands; and finally var. *intercedens*, with broad ovate leaves, narrow at the tip, whitish beneath with coarse teeth, white flowers.

Personal experience as well as observation of others in the Eastern area indicates that these Japanese species and varieties are not as adaptable and hardy as the United States natives. While many of the Japanese forms are in woods in the mountains, others have been observed and photographed in open alpine regions where they enjoy complete exposure to sun. Most of these areas are cool in summer, with much humidity, and winters provide substantial snow cover. This combination of elements explains the difficulty in establishing these handsome plants in the East where there are hot summers and unreliable snowcover in the winter. In the more equitable climate of the Pacific Northwest, these Japanese species appear to be more adaptable, and some impressive plantings of them have been observed in gardens in that area. In Great Britain, the general opinion is that the Japanese species are more adaptable to their climate than the American ones.

Jefferson diphylla (Twin leaf) was formerly known by the cumbersome genus, *Plagiorhegma*. It is an easy plant with distinctive foliage, deeply cleft into two lobes producing individual one-inch white flowers in March or April.

Jeffersonia dubia is the only other species, and is native to Manchurian woods, indicating a remarkable geographical distribution for this genus. This is the more beautiful plant, large lavender-blue flowers following the unfolding metallic blue-green leaves in early April. The foliage gradually turns green as it matures. Both species self-sow when planted in proper woodland conditions, humus-enriched soil which retains moisture.

In the study of the comparative flora of eastern Asia and eastern North America, there are other genera distributed within and outside Japan, which have also proven to be choice plants adaptable to our climate. The following are some that are particularly desirable for shade.

Pachysandra procumbens

This native from southeast United States, although introduced into cultivation in 1800 and described and illustrated in color in the Botanical Register in its first volume in 1815, is not well known nor readily available. Its description varies from semi-herbaceous to semi-woody or half-evergreen, but in the New York suburbs the foliage is usually mutilated by winter conditions, and thus should be sheared in early spring before the new growth emerges. The foliage is dull and slightly pubescent, and is clustered at the top of the 8- to 12-inch stem. The 4-inch flower stalk is produced from the base of the stem. Although a coarse ground cover, it is useful even in deep shade and under adverse conditions. Its best demonstrated use is as an extensive, lush ground cover under the low-hanging branches of a huge beech tree—always a difficult area where there are few possible candidates for an effective long-lived planting.

Pachysandra terminalis

First introduced into Europe in 1882 from Japan where it is widely distributed in woods in lowlands and low mountains in all the five major islands, this coarse plant with its evergreen foliage is familiar to most gardeners in the East, where it is perhaps the most overused ground cover. Its varying uses are easily demonstrated by a drive through the suburban areas. But it is interesting to note that at great contrast to its popularity and adaptability here, there has not been extensive use of it in Great Britain and on the Continent. Even in Japan the average small garden cannot cope with this aggressive plant, which can eventually overtake and smother its near companions.

Although the records indicate about five species of this genus, the only other known in cultivation is *P. axillaris*, a native of China and introduced in 1901 by E. H. Wilson. Although an evergreen, it does not retain this condition in our climate. Experience has proven that it is a much slower grower here, and the foliage is usually damaged in winter even if in deep shade and protection.

Below: Saxifraga stolonifera
Right: Iris cristata 'Alba'

Iris gracilipes

This iris is native to mountain areas from the southern to northern islands of Japan. The huge *Iris* genus is divided into eleven groups, each with common characters. One, is the Evansia group and includes this choice Japanese species, as well as two eastern U.S. species which are also being mentioned. This group was named after Thomas Evans, who introduced the tallest, *I. japonica*, which is questionably hardy. *Iris gracilipes* forms a slender, creeping rhizome with fan-shaped leaves 10 inches long. From this dense neat foliage appear branched and wiry stems, bearing dainty round flowers of pale lilac with orange crests. It is a plant for partial shade, appreciating an open woodland soil. It is a fine companion with the following two species.

Iris cristata

This is the eastern U.S. species in the Evansia group. It is more spreading in habit and is excellent for retaining shady slopes. It is smaller in stature than the preceding species, with wider and shorter foliage. The single flowers on 6-inch stems vary in shades of lilac, blue or mauve, and occasionally a deeper color form is available. It is an excellent ground cover for partial shade and will multiply rapidly in light woodland soil.

Iris lacustris is native to shores of the Great Lakes, which still makes it an Eastern species. It is the most diminutive of the three. Resembling a miniature form of *I. cristata*, it was for a period considered a variety of it, but it is definitely a separate species. The similar flowers are individually borne an inch or two high. There is also some color variation in these appealing flowers. Cultivation should be in sandy or gritty soil with some humus. All three of the described iris have albino forms, which are generally available, except for *I. lacustris alba*, a comparatively rare form and seldom offered in the nursery trade.

Saxifrages for Shade

The saxifrage family includes over 300 species with widely varying cultural requirements. This genus is divided into about 16 different sections; the one deserving attention here is the Diptera group. It has been selected because of the adaptability of most of its species to shade gardening. The group consists of only about six species, all native to China and Japan. No North American species are represented. All the following Japanese species have proven dependable in this area for the shady garden.

Saxifraga stolonifera has been known erroneously as *S. sarmentosa*, with the vernacular names of mother-of-thousands, Aaron's beard, strawberry-geranium and others. The species was first introduced into cultivation from China in the late 18th century and during all the intervening years, it has been cultivated primarily as a house plant. Many garden visitors here appear startled to observe the plant spreading on moss-covered rocks along pools, and its ability to endure the winter climate. This type of habitat is similar to its native conditions in Japan. It may also be used as a spreading ground cover in damp shady woodlands. The round marbled foliage is variable in coloring. It produces numerous creeping red stolons bearing young plants which easily root into available moss, open soil or crevices. The 10- to 12-inch branching flower spikes of mid-summer bear quantities of attractive white, irregularly shaped petals with some red spotting.

81

Saxifraga fortunei, while native to various Japanese mountain areas, also spreads into Korea, Manchuria and China. It is a very hardy deciduous plant, forming clumps without stolons, preferring shady protected areas. It has handsome large, glossy leathery foliage. Its 12- to 15-inch flower spike, produced in October, bears pure white, irregular petalled flowers.

Note from the Editor: *Saxifraga fortunei* is now classified as a variety of *S. cortusifolia*. The undersides of its leaves are maroon-colored, unlike the species, and its foliage has longer and denser hairs and is unusually deeply cleft. It also preceeds the species in bloom by about a month

The nativity of *Saxifraga cortusifolia* is in question; some references state China and others Japan, but apparently it is an Asian species. This plant may be described as a diminutive form of *S. stolonifera* with similar variegated coloring and stoloniferous habit. The flower structure is also reduced in size with 3-inch spikes. It is definitely an indoor plant in this climate (or even in more temperate areas), for repeated efforts to cultivate it outdoors with various protecting means have proved unsuccessful. A cool greenhouse is its ideal winter home.

Saxifraga veitchiana is another member of the Diptera group, a native of Hupeh in China. The roundish 1-1/2-inch foliage is fleshy and dark green. It is also a stoloniferous plant, producing a dense ground cover in partial shade. It has been extremely hardy, requiring no protection or coddling. The 6- to 9-inch flower panicle, produced in late summer, has the typical irregular petals, pure white.

Primula sieboldii

In a genus of over 200 species throughout the world (primarily in the Northern Hemisphere), Japan is only represented by 13 species. Of these, the most adaptable to our Eastern climate is the very variable *P. sieboldii*. It has proven to be the most permanent of all primrose species and hybrids, tolerating all extremes of this area. Its defensive habit of shedding its foliage when dry or attacked by red spider, and retaining its underground creeping rhizomes, is the secret of its long life and ease of increase. If there were to be a choice of only one primula species for this garden, this is the selected one.

In Japan there is a specialized plant society devoted only to this species, and entire spring shows display many variations of form, color and size. In fact, there are hundreds of named varieties grown by Japanese specialists of this species. The plant has soft crinkled foliage from which rise 8- to 10-inch flower spikes. These run the gamut from pure white, pink, rose and lavender, to bluish, but not yellow. The outlines of the petals are as variable as snow flakes. It may be of interest to note that double forms have not been introduced. Its cultural requirements are simple—part shade, moist root run and care in not disturbing the dormant rhizomes. Where conditions are satisfactory, self-sown seedlings will appear. Propagation from seed usually produces a variable group of interesting plants.

Menziesia purpurea

Japan contains an enormous collection of deciduous and evergreen ericaceous plants. A lesser-known genus is *Menziesia*, which includes about seven species, all deciduous. Four are in Japan, two in western North America, and one in eastern United States. The American species are not impressive and certainly not garden worthy when compared with those of Japan, which are beautiful plants of slow growth and deserving of representation in any collection. The Japanese species selected for description is undoubtedly the finest, and is not too different from *M. ciliicalyx* (and its varieties), the latter usually being the more dwarf. Other differences are basically botanical. Either species, when available, is worthy of acquisition. The plants and flowers resemble the better-known, closely related genus, *Enkianthus*, but the species of *Menziesia* are more dwarf and slower growers. The urn-shaped flowers of both are in drooping terminal clusters. *M. purpurea* has rich red to deep purple flowers. Its scarcity in commercial channels is regretted and should be corrected.

Leucothoe keiskei

The hardy species of *Leucothoe* are represented in Japan, and both the eastern and western United States. But this selected dwarf Japanese mountain plant has the largest flowers of all the hardy species. It is a beautiful and distinct low, procumbent evergreen shrub with smooth red young wood and glossy bright green foliage. The flowers produced in July are pure white cylinders, 1/2 to 3/4 inch long by 1/4 inch wide, in terminal drooping clusters. It is advisable to plant this species in peaty woodland soil in considerable shade, preferably with a western to northwestern exposure in order to avoid leaf desiccation from cold winter winds. There is also a more diminutive form of this species, but is seldom available.

Pieris nana

This species was formerly included in the now mainly dejunct pic genus, *Arcterica*. It is a diminutive Asiatic shrublet, ranging from northern Japan and areas farther north. It has dense, wiry stems with dark glossy green, leathery leaves. The fragrant flowers are white, roundish urns in terminal clusters of three or four, and open in late April or May. It succeeds in acid, peaty soil and partial shade, and ordinarily is not difficult. It is the perfect plant for the small, shady rock garden, where it can never become a nuisance. Again it is not commonly available.

PLANTS NATIVE ONLY TO JAPAN

In contrast to the preceding there are a number of endemic herbaceous genera in the temperate areas of Japan which are not found elsewhere. They are all worthy plants, ideal for our gardens particularly in shade.

Anemonopsis macrophylla

This distinctive species is comparatively rare in mountain woods on Honshu, the major island of Japan. It is an elegant plant, with foliage resembling *Cimicifuga* and with racemes, about 18 inches high, bearing nodding flowers of waxy texture and icy lavender-blue color. It has proven adaptable to a variety of situations in deep or light shade, and in woodland soil containing much humus—peat moss—to retain moisture. It commences flowering in August and continues through September. It is an easy perennial, long lived and readily (but slowly) grown from seed.

Deinanthe bifida

This Japanese endemic species grows in mountain woodlands in the warmer areas but is dependably hardy in the New York region. It has creeping rhizomes with erect leafy stems up to 2 feet, which bear waxy white flowers in July and August. It prospers in a shaded woodland area among low shrubs.

There is only one other species in eastern Asia, *Deinanthe caerulea*, introduced into cultivation by E. H. Wilson, who sent seed from Hupeh in China. This is another shade-loving woodland plant thriving in damp, peaty woodland soil. It grows to about 12 inches high with foliage like a hydrangea, producing magnificent, lilac-blue nodding and cup-shaped flowers in July and August. Both species have proven hardy for many years in the New York area.

Glaucidium palmatum

This is a distinctive monotypic plant of woods and thickets in high mountains of northern Japan. Being deciduous, its handsome bold foliage rises from the soil in April, gradually unfolding and producing the tight flower buds. The open cup-shaped flowers, 4 to 5 inches in diameter, have a satiny sheen and are lilac-blue in color, shading into white in the center, and set off by a large cluster of golden stamens which enhances the beauty of this wonderful plant. The fully unfolded leaves are broadly palmate and dissected into seven sharply toothed lobes. After fertilization, the flower sets two large bean-like pods containing flat winged seeds, which usually take two years to germinate. The leaves and seed pods do not ripen in very shaded areas until late October. There is a magnificent pure white form, exceedingly rare, and which warrants all effort to locate.

Hakonechloa macra

This monotypic perennial grass, which also has been known as *Phragmites macra*, was seldom seen outside Japan. It has creeping rhizomes with leaf blades from 6 to 10 inches long. It occurs on wet, rocky cliffs in mountains and is rather rare. Its variegated forms are cultivated as ornamental pot plants. In the garden it is an interesting accent in a mixed border and can be used to brighten a shady corner.

Kirengeshoma palmata

Here is another woodland plant of the mountains well suited for a shady slope. Its somewhat palmate leaves are large for the 3-foot plant. The flowers, which slowly emerge in August, persist for several weeks, and are 2-inch waxy yellow, pendent bells of great charm. It is an easy, long-lived shade plant, easily propagated by division, cuttings and seed. Why has such a dramatic plant remained so rare?

Tanakaea radicans

This evergreen perennial is not completely endemic to Japan as it does spread into China. It is comparatively rare in its native habitat, wet, shady rocks where it gradually covers the moss and soil with its delicate growth. The leaves, pointed, toothed, deep green and leathery, produce erect white plumes of flowers, about 5 inches high, and indicate its close relationship to the astilbes. From each crown, fine stolons or runners emerge, and small plants are then produced from their tips, so that there is a slow radiating increase of this dainty ground cover. The growth is not excessive because of its size and slow rate of increase. It is an ideal plant when placed in the shade produced by choice, small ericaceous plants.

These choice Japanese and Asiatic herbaceous and woody plants are only a small sampling of the jewels available from that area of the world for the shady garden. Are there not sufficient keen and selective gardeners who appreciate these treasures of nature? Why do the introduction and commercial availability of the finer species require generations before being acknowledged and offered? In 1911 Reginald Farrer, the English dean of rock gardening, stated in his book *My Rock Garden,* "*Saxifraga fortunei* is a singularly beautiful species, far too little cultivated." This was expressed 58 years ago and, while many of the recommended species are available in Great Britain, their availability remains limited in the United States. ❖

TREES AND SHRUBS FOR SPECIAL EFFECTS

FREDERICK MCGOURTY, JR.

Kerria japonica 'Pleniflora' blooms well in substantial shade.

Gardeners who are very fond of showy flowering shrubs and trees are often disappointed with shady gardens, but there are several blessings to such sites. Actually, the flowering time of most woody plants is only about ten days a year, depending on weather conditions. Unfortunately, many of the commonly planted flowering trees and shrubs, which usually require full or nearly full sun, have little merit aside from their blooms. This means that about 355 days of the year are frequently endured with a monotonous landscape.

Yet, some of the plants that are attractive year-round are not especially ornamental in flower. When leaf texture, twig color and bark character are considered, the horizons of the shady garden widen. A number of broad-leaved evergreens, including ones of border-line hardiness, come to their best in gardens that receive some winter shade, and most variegated plants, which can provide flower-like relief in deep green areas of the garden, can be grown well only in partial shade in areas of the country where the summer sun is severe.

For brilliant stem color in winter, when gardens are often drab, the Siberian dogwood (*Cornus alba* 'Sibirica') and yellow-twig dogwood (*C. sericea* 'Flaviramea') can brighten northern gardens that are shaded by deciduous trees. These shrubs are most attractive in snow, but they should be pruned severely in early spring to assure vigorous new growth. It is only the young wood of the previous season or two that is vividly colored. *Kerria japonica*, a green-twig shrub that blooms well in substantial shade may serve as a good complement to the dogwoods for a winter effect. The etiolated growth common to shady areas may be turned to advantage with these shrubs.

The cinnamon-colored bark of two species of *Clethra*, *C. acuminata* and *C. barbinervis*, is most attractive in winter. Both are hardy as far north as New England. These large-growing shrubs or small trees have more character than the summer-sweet (*C. alnifolia*), which is often grown in shady gardens for its fragrant flowers. The latter has undistinguished stems and

becomes leggy unless the old wood is cut out from the base periodically.

The striped-bark maple (*Acer pensylvanicum*) is not common in gardens, but its winter effect can be superb in the cool northern states. This tree of small eventual height thrives in shady spots in woodsy soil. The more vigorously it grows, the more pronounced the green and white striped bark will be.

One of the most distinctive tall growing shrubs for twig character is the winged euonymus (*Euonymus alatus*). While its flowers are inconspicuous, it is shade-tolerant, and the winged stems do not appear as pronounced in the compact form ('Compactus'), which makes a fine hedge where euonymus scale is not a problem. Burning-bush is an appropriate name for this plant, for the autumn color is probably the most intense red of any hardy shrub.

Apart from rhododendrons and the many varieties of azaleas that retain their foliage over winter, there are numerous broad-leaved evergreens that grow well in the North with some winter shade. While in the South some of the following shrubs may appear at their best in full sun, they are best grown in the New York area in some winter shade to minimize tip injury. A brief list of border-line species on Long Island benefiting from shade would include *Aucuba japonica, Camellia japonica,* English holly (*Ilex aquifolium*), Chinese holly (*I. cornuta*), Japanese privet (*Ligustrum japonicum*), glossy privet (*L. lucidum*) and *Osmanthus heterophyllus* (*ilicifolius*). This list becomes more impressive when one remembers that there are a large number of garden varieties of each of these plants.

Even Japanese holly (*Ilex crenata*), which

is rather dependably hardy in New York City, may occasionally suffer winter leaf injury if planted in full sun. This is especially true of *I.c.* 'Convexa.' The evergreen Oregon-grape (*Mahonia aquifolium*) and its relatives demand a good degree of shade in the colder months here. Some of the evergreen barberries (*Berberis julianae, B. triacanthophora* and *B. verruculosa*) also appear to grow best in some shade, at least until they are fully established.

Mention should be given Reeves skimmia (*Skimmia reevesiana*), a low-growing member of the citrus family. Under the dense shade of Austrian pines in the Rock Garden at the Brooklyn Botanic Garden, this shrub, used as ground cover, always attracts attention. For a good part of the year it has red holly-like fruit. The somewhat taller-growing *Skimmia japonica*, which is only slightly less desirable because it is dioecious, also benefits from shade. When grown in full sun, these shrubs will often suffer winter injury in New York.

Shrubs and trees with variegated foliage are more popular in England and in the Pacific Northwest than they are in the Northeast. One reason for this may be climatic, since the relatively weak rays of the sun in more evenly moist climates permits these plants to be grown under a variety of circumstances. In the Northeast, unless variegated shrubs are given partial shade, their leaves frequently burn. While their excessive use can be hideous, an occasional planting in a shaded area may provide much needed contrast—almost a flowering effect. Among the best woody plants with variegated leaves are *Kerria japonica* 'Picta,' tricolor dogwood (*Cornus florida* 'Welchii'), silver-edged shrubby dogwood (*C. alba* 'Argenteo-marginata'), the Drummond or Harlequin form of Norway maple (*Acer platanoides* 'Drummondii'), tricolor beech (*Fagus sylvatica* 'Tricolor') and gold-dust shrub (*Aucuba japonica* 'Variegata'). The last is often grown as a house plant, but it is hardy outdoors in a shaded spot as far north as N.Y. City.

Several members of the witch-hazel family are valuable in shady gardens for their distinctive foliage as well as their flowers. *Corylopsis pauciflora*, a dense low-growing shrub, has delicately pleated leaves, while the taller (to about 6 feet or so) *Corylopsis sinensis*, which has an open growth habit, has leaves with a bluish cast. Both have yellow flowers about the time forsythia is in bloom. *Fothergilla gardenii*, to 3 feet, and the taller *Fothergilla major* have leaves that somewhat resemble witch-hazel. The autumn coloration is often a fine red, while the flowers, which look like small bottle-brushes, are attractive in partly shaded areas of the garden in early May.

Occasionally, a coarse leaf effect may be desired to break the monotony of a shady spot. Oak-leaf hydrangea (*Hydrangea quercifolia*), leather-leaf mahonia (*Mahonia bealei*) and leather-leaf viburnum (*Viburnum rhytidophyllum*) can provide a good contrast when planted with narrow-leaved shrubs. Among the latter might be the weeping English yew (*Taxus baccata* 'Repandens'), dwarf Japanese yew (*Taxus cuspidata nana*) or shrubby forms of common hemlock (*Tsuga canadensis*). ❖

FREDERICK MCGOURTY, JR. *was formerly the editor of* Plants & Gardens. *He and his wife run a nursery for perennials in Connecticut.*

SHADE AND ORNAMENTAL TREES

RICHARD WALTER

To one who has spent many years in a suburban community as a municipal arborist, garden adviser, teacher and patient listener to garden problems, the list of tree worries seems to be endless and so often a convenient place to put all sorts of garden failures to rest. Over the years I have become very critical about the selection and use of trees, not only by municipal tree planters, but also by those who plant on private property.

Light to medium shade can be very desirable and beneficial to our gardens and for our comfort. When trees, by their numbers, by the density of the shade they cast and by their root activity, make it impossible for other plant material to thrive under or near them, then the trees become the destroying agents of our gardens and the real estate they represent. In every municipality, such hopeless and degenerating gardens can be found. When they multiply, the desirability and values drop with all the symptoms of a declining neighborhood.

Most people are naturally sentimental about trees and hesitate to accuse trees of robbing them of the full enjoyment of their gardens. Actually nature never created a bad tree but assigned each one to its specific place. So the trouble is caused by those who

RICHARD WALTER, *Maplewood, New Jersey, has recently retired as supervisor of the Parks and Shade Tree Department there. A long-time member of the New Jersey Federation of Shade Tree Commissions, he has many interests, including the development of vegetable-growing as a fine art.*

select and plant trees, and when mistakes are made, they last a long time and the expenses to correct them grow with the trees.

Tree selection and planting are a serious business. Of course, it is not always the killing shade which causes other plant life to fail under trees. Shallow and aggressive root systems of some species do this very effectively. A few, like the black walnut, may even poison the soil for many other plants. Then the depletion of nutrients and of decomposable organic matter, diminishing water-holding capacity, and soil compaction can destroy most other plants under the trees. Most often a combination of these evils will lead to an abandoned garden. Yet shade—the right amount of it—from high branches and deep-rooted trees can lend much to the full enjoyment of a garden and to the environment of a community. When those trees are further enhanced by showy flowers, fruits or foliage, then they become a gardener's delight. What gardener does not dream of having once the opportunity to

Flowering dogwood, Cornus florida, can be trained into an informal standard by pruning the lower branches.

plant the right trees in the right places ideal for sun-loving and shade-loving plants, for roses and rhododendrons, for chrysanthemums and ferns.

Too often when this opportunity arises for the home gardener or the town planter they panic and plant for quick shade and the most

shade. They plant fast-growing, shallow-rooted, and heavy shading trees and plant five where one should be enough.

Among the wide selection of desirable, amenable trees are those of large, medium and small sizes. The spacing of trees is best determined by getting acquainted with the average mature spread of the particular species or variety. This spread, plus a little extra for the sun to reach down into the garden, becomes the guide line for spacing. Thus sugar maple, with an average spread of 40 feet, should be given at least 50 to 60 feet of spacing, a red or white oak, 60 to 70 feet, while small trees, like Siberian crab apple, dogwood, hawthorn rarely spread over 25 feet and can be spaced 30 to 35 feet apart. A backyard of about 50 by 50 feet cannot have two or more large trees, but it can have one large and two or three small trees. It is almost the rule in street tree planting to find on a 50-foot frontage, two maples or lindens or planes or pin oaks, naturally with disastrous results to plantings, utility installations, sidewalks and curbs.

A trick to make many of the small trees more suitable as flowering shade trees is a practice known as form-training. This is pruning back of the lower side branches. As the young tree grows either in the nursery or at the planting site, this pruning is continued until a sturdy trunk is formed 6- to 8-feet high and the crown is shaped. Then all stubs of the former lower side branches are removed. A dogwood, hawthorn or crab apple can be form trained into a flowering shade tree. Arboretums and display gardens often show such trees as they naturally grow, like oversized shrubs, unpruned, unshaped, with very little practical garden use. Fine examples of this form-training are the American holly trees on the terrace at Longwood Gardens.

Small flowering trees, trained by pruning into standard trees, are becoming very popular for mall and street planting, and are equally well suited for home gardens. Certainly one man's opinion must never be used as a sole yard stick here, but it can serve as a starting point in tree evaluation. First consideration in tree selection is tolerance to soil conditions and compatibility towards other plants under or near it; then its behavior above and below ground in relation to structures and installations; depth of root systems; ornamental value; structural strength; resistance to insects and diseases; litter problem and recovery from transplanting. Least important should be cost. Some trees have more desirable qualities than others. The space in a garden is valuable and only the best qualified plants should be chosen.

LARGE SHADE TREES

Oaks: Most tolerant, and top selections are the red, scarlet, black and white oaks, if given proper spacing and lower branches are removed. Lesser known is the saw tooth oak, very open headed, tolerant to various soil conditions and compatible with other plants. Least wanted is the pin oak, *Quercus palustris,* and the similar willow oak. Both are shallow-rooted and, therefore, not compatible with other plants. They rate as high-maintenance trees.

Maples: Among them the sugar maple is truly a magnificent tree where space is adequate. Deep rooted, compatible with other plants if lower branches are removed to a height of 12-15 feet. **CAUTION**: Sugar maples will not tolerate poorly drained, compacted soils or polluted air. *Acer rubrum,* the red maple, deserves consideration as a lawn tree, though it is shallow-rooted and less compatible with other plants. The nursery trade offers several selected clones with improved autumn color, conical and narrow columnar forms. These varied selections of red maple plus tolerance for thriving on shallow soil often make them a good choice. Least compatible to other plants are the many forms of the Norway maples, except the columnar form. For the same reason one should be critical of silver maple, plane-tree maple, and boxelder, except perhaps on seashore or city locations, where other trees have a difficult time.

Honey Locust: Much credit should be given to the nurserymen who now offer improved clones of honey locust far superior to the species. These honey locusts are large trees, both in spread and height, and are very compatible with other plants, as well as tolerant of soil and location and cause very little litter. However, there are no showy features of flowers, fruit or autumn color and there can be troubles from pests. It also appears that these honey locusts will be overplanted for the same reasons as are Norway maples, pin oaks or plane trees and that is, easy and quick nursery propagation and quick recovery after transplanting.

I dare here to list the black locust (*Robinia*) as a ruggedly beautiful native tree. Its faults are a poor root system, ground suckering and pests. Its place is in mixed screen plantings on banks or marginal planting areas.

Elms: Some day we all hope to plant the American elm again as it is the finest large tree. Its cousin, the zelkova, is hardly a substitute, although it is a neat, open-headed tree to supply light shade. It is resistant to Dutch elm disease, but not the elm leaf beetle.

Yellow-wood: A most beautiful and little-known large native, big tree, yellow-wood (*Cladrastis lutea*), is deep rooted and compatible with other plants if lower branches are removed. Tolerant of poor soil, but recovery from transplanting can be a little slow. It is best moved in the spring with a root ball. A little patience and skill are needed in the nursery and later, on the planting site, to shape it to standard tree form. This difficulty may also account for its unpopularity with nurserymen. Select a planting site for its ultimate size of approximately a 30- to 40-foot spread and height of about 50 to 60 feet. It does make a big tree.

Callery Pear (Pyrus calleryana): A very popular tree in the medium-to-large range; valuable as a street and park tree and highly recommended for home gardens. Our first plantings, about 20 years old, are nearly 30 feet high with 10- to 12-inch diameter trunks. Very deep rooted, compatible and soil-tolerant, almost pest free, good foliage, showy with its white flowers and autumn color. The clone 'Bradford' is nearly non-fruiting. Our seedling selections produce some fruit less than 1/2 inch in diameter, which are readily taken by birds during the winter months. It will grow to 40 feet in height and has a 30-foot spread.

Scholar Tree (Sophora japonica): Under favorable growing conditions and in about 50 years, this tree can reach a height of 60 to 70 feet and spread of 40 feet. Travelers through France in August can spot it by the white clouds of flowers reaching over the tree line of villages and towns. It is very compatible with other plants, gives light shade, and is deep rooted and showy. Pest-free but sensitive to wet, shallow, compacted and sour soil conditions with die-back or total loss of the trees often resulting. CAUTION: Flower and fruit litter can become a nuisance. Plant away from heavily used walks or patios.

Dawn Redwood (Metasequoia glyptostroboides): A non-evergreen conifer and the most exciting and most promising of the newer introduced trees for streets, parks and home gardens. Most significant is the fact that the heavy and irregular butt swelling of this tree almost never appears when it is grown

as a standard tree with the lower branches removed in the nursery or in the planting site to a height of 7 to 9 feet. Deep rooted, very compatible and tolerant. No leaf litter and good yellow autumn color; it can be pruned and shaped at will and transplants readily bare root, either in fall or spring. Recovery and growth are rapid. It may tend to be over-flexible while young, but will become sturdy and strong as it matures. It is a big tree and should reach 50 or more feet with a 25- to 30-foot spread.

THE SMALLER TREES

With properties becoming smaller, tree-growing spaces on the streets steadily shrinking and tree care getting more expensive, the search is on for smaller trees as shown by the widening choices in nursery catalogs. These trees are difficult and costly to produce, are usually in short supply, and may have to be ordered years ahead of delivery.

Crab Apples: Only the Siberian crab apple, *Malus baccata*, qualifies as a flowering shade tree both for street planting and for home landscaping. It shapes readily into a well-formed standard tree with trunk height of 7 to 8 feet. Height and spread are within about 30 feet. The root system is deep and strong, the tree is compatible and soil-tolerant, with no insect and disease problems. Flowers are white to pink and profuse. CAUTION: Select or purchase only available selections with fruit less than 1/2 inch in diameter. Here, as in the case of the Callery pear, the breakoff point in fruit size is 1/2 inch in diameter. Smaller fruits add to the ornamental value and are bird food. Larger fruits cause a nuisance when dropping. Truly a remarkable small, flowering shade tree, particularly if yellow- or red-fruited. There is also available a very narrow upright form of the Siberian crab apple, dependable and tolerant as a standard or a flowering tree, high narrow hedge or screen.

The Dogwoods: Their potential value as ornamental trees has hardly been discovered for municipal and business-area landscaping. In home gardens we find the dogwoods either as part of the screen planting or as oversized treelike shrubs, branched close to the ground and taking up as much as several hundred square feet of garden space. The native dogwood, *Cornus florida*, and the pink-flowering forms readily respond to form-training in the nursery or at the planting location to become small standard trees. Spring bulbs, some perennials, ground covers and turf can then be established and maintained under them. Add to this a garden bench and you have a feature without equal when the tree is in bloom or in its autumn color.

Cornus florida, when trained as a standard tree, makes a good choice for inter-planting with larger trees along streets of suburban developments, and the same form is ideal for mall or walk planting where good growing conditions can be maintained. Dogwood enthusiasts will find some excellent new improved varieties with larger white flowers or deeper pink flowers, with double flowers and either reddish or variegated foliage. Keep these in mind when choosing dogwoods.

Cornus kousa, the Japanese dogwood, makes its own show about two weeks later and is excitingly beautiful. But this tree resists form-pruning and is best grown as a low-branched or half-standard tree. My efforts to shape this dogwood to standard form failed. Either they persisted in heavy suckering from the base or the top branches stunted. In fact the general growth of this dogwood is more typical of a large shrub.

The rare *Cornus controversa* must be mentioned. It is a medium-size tree, shaping up readily to a good formal branch structure. The flowers somewhat resemble those of "Queen Ann's Lace." It is not as showy as the others. We found it quickly in trouble when not regularly watered the first year after transplanting. To this I must add that the professional plantsman and the home gardener should be aware that all dogwoods are quickly discouraged by poor location, by competition with aggressive trees and particularly by neglect.

Dogwoods are shallow rooted, sensitive to overheating and compacting soil, low fertility or strong chemical fertilizers and easily injured by drought. We get best results by broadcasting Hollytone, a fertilizer high in cottonseed meal, under the trees in the fall, and adding 2 inches of old woodchips or leafmold as mulch. The fertilizer is calibrated at about 2 lbs. per one-inch trunk diameter. Borer infestations often follow exposure and drought. Creating the best growing conditions is far more effective than chemical control.

Editor's Note: Gardeners should be aware that in ecent years dogwood anthracnose, or lower branch dieback, has been a problem for *Cornus florida*, the native dogwood. *Cornus kousa*, once considered resistant, is now showing symptoms of the disease as well.

Flowering Cherries: Here it is more difficult to pick out the best for street, garden and mall planting. Generally the Kwanzan is first choice, being the most spectacular in flower, and also it is readily produced to standard form in the nursery. We prefer the single cherries, the Yoshino, the Higans and the Sargent. Durable, fairly deep rooted, compatible but requiring good soil conditions. Leaf rust, scale and borer insects must be watched. Yoshino and Sargent cherry have a 30- to 35-foot spread; the Higans cherry, 25 to 30 feet.

Hawthorns: Outstanding is the Lavalle hawthorn, a hybrid from France, widely used in Europe as a street, small garden and mall tree. It should do very well in large planters. Very adaptable to our climate; it is clean, deep-rooted, compatible, very tolerant and rarely troubled by pests and smog. It is drought resistant. Flowers, foliage and fruit are all very ornamental. It rarely exceeds 25 feet in height and spread with a trunk diameter of 10 to 12 inches. As it is easily shaped and long lived, it qualifies for the small garden, in business and municipal landscaping and as a street tree. Very few of our nurseries make the effort to grow the Lavalle hawthorn as a standard tree form, which it will readily do. There are other hawthorns including some very promising new introductions.

Goldenrain Tree (*Koelreuteria paniculata*):
If one looks for exotic features in a tree, then this one should satisfy. It has beautiful flowers in midsummer when color is scarce among trees. Very interesting are the Japanese-lanternlike seedpods appearing later, first light green and finally a glossy brown. Not too easily grown with a straight trunk as it takes more nursery and pruning at planting to shape a good crown 8 to 9 feet above ground level. A very deep-

rooted, drought-resistant, compatible tree, but it should have good soil. It is a conversation piece in any garden and does very well as a flowering street tree.

This list of recommendations is already lengthy, yet many fine trees are not mentioned. However, we must not overlook the Turkish hazelnut tree, *Corylus colurna*. It is still a rare tree, but appears to be very well suited for the small-to-medium garden. It is a very handsome tree in summer and winter. ❖

A flowering 'Kwanzan' cherry in full bloom.

INSECT RESISTANT SHRUBS

RICHARD J. GOUGER

Some of the most attractive shrubs recommended for shade are unfortunately susceptible to insect invasions. Many pests fall into the nuisance category, but others can be serious enough to make the homeowner avoid the plants they prey upon and where practical consider substitution of less susceptible subjects. However, rarely do all the pests associated with a plant or group of plants appear at once, and sometimes never, especially around home grounds. Therefore, even those plants which are hosts to many pests (see table which follows) can be grown successfully. As a safeguard, they can be sprayed two or three times a season with the recommended chemicals (always follow directions). It would be ideal if such plants as flowering dogwood, rhododendron and azalea—three of the most suitable as well as most beautiful of plants recommended for shaded gardens, but also host to several kinds of pests—had resistant counterparts equally as beautiful.

The following table has been prepared as an indication of susceptibility to insect attack of the various shrubs commonly grown in shade. The figures under relative susceptibility indicate the degree of immunity, plants having the higher numbers (3-4-5) being usually less susceptible to insect injury.

Diseases and other factors should also be considered in selection of shrubs for shady places. It is of interest that some of the insects listed, lace bugs for example, are rarely found in shade in large numbers so, while they cannot be excluded, do not constitute an important consideration when selecting shrubs for shade. In fact, lace bugs, which can disfigure or seriously damage andromeda (*Pieris*) when it is grown in sunshine, virtually disappear when the same plant is moved into shaded or partially shaded locations.

Witch-hazel
Hamamelis virginiana

RICHARD J. GOUGER. *At the time his article was written, he was Entomologist at the Bartlett Tree Research Laboratories, Charlotte, North Carolina.*

Relative Susceptibility
of Shade-Tolerant Shrubs
to Insect Pest Damage

Host	Relative Susceptibility	Insects
(Shrubs having the higher numbers should be given preference by insect-conscious gardeners)		
Acanthopanax sieboldianus Fiveleaf Aralia	5	Four-lined Plant Bug
Amelanchier (Various) Shadblow	1	Wooly Elm Aphid Borers Oystershell Scale Pear-slug Sawfly
Aronia (Various) Chokeberry	5	Roundheaded Apple Tree Borer
Azalea	1	Azalea Stem Borer Rhododendron Borer Lace Bug Leaf Miner Mites Azalea Bark Scale Soft Azalea Scale Black Vine Weevil
Berberis thunbergii Japanese Barberry	3	Barberry Aphid Barberry Scale Barberry Webworm Japanese Weevil
Buxus (Various) Boxwood	2	Boxwood Leaf Miner Boxwood Mite Boxwood Psyllid
Ceanothus americanus Jersey-tea	4	Ceanothus Aphid Ceanothus Lace Bug San Jose Scale
Cephalanthus occidentalis Buttonbush	4	San Jose Scale
Cornus (Various) Dogwood	1	Borers Leafhoppers Dogwood Scale
Euonymus fortunei Wintercreeper	1	Green Peach Aphid Euonymus Scale
Forsythia (Various) Goldenbells	5	Four-lined Plant Bug
Hamamelis virginiana Witch-hazel	5	Saddle Prominent Caterpillar Witch-hazel Cone Gall
Hydrangea (Various)	3	Aphids & Mites Rose Chafer Hydrangea Leaf Tier

Host	Relative Susceptibility	Insects
Ilex crenata Japanese Holly	3	Leaf Miners Mites
Kalmia latifolia Mountain-laurel	2	Azalea Stem Borer Rhododendron Borer Lace Bugs
Ligustrum (Various) Privet	3	Lilac Borer Privet Thrips Greenhouse Whitefly
Lonicera morrowii Morrow Honeysuckle	2	Honeysuckle Aphid Long-tailed Mealybug Honeysuckle Sawfly Oystershell Scale San Jose Scale
Myrica pensylvanica Northern Bayberry	5	Red-humped Caterpillar
Pieris floribunda Mountain Andromeda	4	Japanese Lace Bug Florida Wax Scale Mites
Rhododendron (Various)	2	Azalea Stem Borer Rhododendron Borer Rhododendron Lace Bug Taxus Root Weevil
Rhus canadensis Fragrant Sumac	2	Sumac Aphid Currant Borer Sumac Psyllid Cottony Maple Scale San Jose Scale
Ribes alpinum Mountain Currant	1	Currant Aphid Currant Borer Imported Currant Worm Sawfly Flatheaded Apple Tree Borer Pacific Flatheaded Borer
Rubus odoratus Flowering Raspberry	1	Raspberry Aphid Borers Mites Strawberry Root Weevil Glacial Whitefly
Sambucus racemosa Red Elder	2	Aphids Elder Borer Currant Borer San Jose Scale
Symphoricarpos albus Snowberry	3	Aphids Snowberry Clearwing Moth San Jose Scale Glacial Whitefly
Viburnum (Various)	2	Aphids Dogwood Twig Borer Mites Scales (Various)